SPLiT

Stories from a Generation Raised on Divorce

Edited by Ava Chin

Contemporary Books

Chicago New York San Francisco Lisbon London Madrid Mexico City
Milan New Delhi San Juan Seoul Singapore Sydney Toronto

Library of Congress Cataloging-in-Publication Data

Split : stories from a generation raised on divorce / edited by Ava Chin.
     p.   cm.
    ISBN 0-07-139106-1
    1. Children of divorced parents—United States.   2. Children of
single parents—United States.   3. Adult children of divorced parents—
United States. I. Chin, Ava.

HQ777.5.S644   2002
306.89—dc21   2002020798

Contemporary Books

A Division of The McGraw·Hill Companies

Some of the names and places within these essays have been changed.

Doug Goetsch's "Wherever You Want" has previously appeared in the magazines *Hanging Loose* (1995), *Wherever You Want* (Pavement Saw Press, 1997), and *Nobody's Hell* (Hanging Loose Press, 1999).

An excerpt of Peppur Chambers's "Three-Way" entitled "Texas" was originally published in *TellSpin* magazine (Spring/Summer 2001).

1 2 3 4 5 6 7 8 9 0   AGM/AGM   1 0 9 8 7 6 5 4 3 2

ISBN 0-07-139106-1

This book was set in Sabon
Printed and bound by Quebecor Martinsburg

Cover design by Monica Baziuk
Cover photograph copyright © David Birschbach
Back-cover author photograph by Mara Faye Lethem

McGraw-Hill books are available at special quantity discounts to use as premiums and sales promotions, or for use in corporate training programs. For more information, please write to the Director of Special Sales, Professional Publishing, McGraw-Hill, Two Penn Plaza, New York, NY 10121-2298. Or contact your local bookstore.

This book is printed on acid-free paper.

CONTENTS

ACKNOWLEDGMENTS

I WISH TO THANK all of those who helped in the making of this book: to my wonderful writers, who were brave and insightful; Katherine Pushkar, a great friend and editor, who was vigilant in her unerring support; my friends Leslie Cribbs, Crystal Williams, Kate Papacosma, Susan Sung-Danelian, and Keith Grant who listened well into the middle of the night; everyone at the Johns Hopkins Writing Seminars, including Jen Starrels, Laura Bajor, Jane Delury, Elisabeth Cohen, and Molly McQuade, among others, as well as professors Judith Grossman and Carol Burke, in whose workshop my essay was first critiqued; Johns Hopkins sociology chair and family expert Andrew Cherlin; everyone who helped with the book in its earliest stages, including Alan Light, Sia Michels, Janice Eidus, Fiona Giles, and Barbara Gogan; friends from the Asian American Writers' Workshop, including Monique T. D. Truong, Quang Bao, and Hanya Yanagihara; my editor, Michele Pezzuti, for her wisdom and insight, and everyone at Contemporary Books/McGraw-Hill, especially Ellen Vinz; my agent, Eileen Cope, for her belief in this anthology; and finally, to my family, especially my mother, grandmother, and the memory of my grandfather.

INTRODUCTION

A FEW YEARS AGO, I was in a television studio with half a dozen other twenty-somethings for the taping of an HBO talk-show pilot. Urban youth of varied ethnicity—students, writers, singers—my peers and I were preparing to talk about issues important to our generation. As we sat on velvety couches arranged in a semicircle and designed to look like a hip living room, the cameras began to roll. Our moderator, a perky former host for MTV, started the discussion off by asking if we thought marriage was still relevant. The overwhelming response was no.

"Marriage is just a contract," said a girl with elaborately cornrowed hair that ended in small braids at her shoulders. "Just because people are married doesn't mean they love each other."

"You could just as easily get divorced," said the lanky English guy sitting next to her, his spiky hair gleaming with gel under the studio lights.

"I'd rather just live with someone," asserted a student in a denim mini-dress sitting cross-legged near me. The English guy smiled and everyone seemed to agree at once. "Why get married?"

As I listened to them support and add to each other's viewpoints, I felt like I was hearing myself at twenty-one. Rational. Defensive. Justified by the statistics. We had seen a marriage or two that worked, but knew far more that hadn't. This was our reality, and reality bit.

But being a few crucial years older and having already considered the idea of marriage and kids for myself, I was flabbergasted. As a child of divorce several times over, I believed in marriage in an unwavering way that my own parents and, apparently, my younger peers did not. As I listened to their excuses for why marriage was meaningless in the wake of a 50 percent divorce rate, the studio lights beamed down and the cameras whirled around us. Finally, the producer held up a sign. "Ask Ava what she thinks."

I was the only one that day who insisted that marriage was not just an antiquated social contract that went out with the 1950s. As a child, I had seen my mother struggle financially and worry needlessly over who was going to love her. I had witnessed my friends negotiate battling parents who after the divorce either didn't talk to each other or continued to fight. For them, there was no central home to go to for holidays, and if their parents remarried, they experienced the continual feeling of being a stranger in somebody else's house.

"I don't know anyone who wants to keep getting married and divorced like our parents did," I said to the silent group of panelists and producers around me. "And despite the divorce rate, or maybe because I lived through it, I believe in marriage even more."

WHEN I WAS GROWING UP in New York in the 1970s, the common thinking about children of divorce, which I heard over and over again from kids my age with parents who were still married was, "Your parents are divorced? You must be spoiled." The idea was that guilt-ridden parents overcompensated by giving their kids whatever they asked for—their own phones, princess beds, televisions in their bedroom—and as a result kids had free reign over curfews and ate dinners of ice cream and pizza every night. Sort of a *Little Lord Fauntleroy* meets *Lord of the Flies* fantasy.

While this may have been true in some cases, it certainly was not for all. Like many children of divorce, I was raised by a mother who struggled to support us on a single salary. There were no outrageous gifts and outlandish spending, no weekend doting and overindulgences. Instead, there were legal battles with my father over child support. There was the kind of tension and fighting that erupts within a family when money is an issue and a parent needs to run the entire household on a thin paycheck. And back then, despite the record numbers of families splitting, there was still a stigma surrounding divorce.

Then the era that ushered in no-fault divorce legislation in 1970 and saw the rise of divorce in record numbers finally gave way to a new wave of conservatism. Under the guise of "family values," right-wing politicians in the 1980s and 1990s lamented the "destruction" of the American family. As a child of divorce, it was difficult for me to hear the dire projections by "experts" about my demographic—apparently we were more likely to drop out of high school, to become depressed, to have a teenage pregnancy, and, as adults, to become divorced parents ourselves. I was angry at these statistics, which did nothing to illuminate the situation of millions of kids my age. I knew many who defied the stereotype, who didn't drop out of school and who were in fact straight-A students but who were nonetheless profoundly affected by divorce in ways that weren't making national headlines.

In putting together this book, I wanted to finally reveal what it was like for us, the first generation that grew up in divorced families en masse. I wanted to hear from the very generation that until now had remained silent. What was it like for them to watch their home life split in two? How did they juggle their relationship with parents who were learning to fly solo again, many of whom later remarried? And now in their twenties and thirties, what were their takes on love and marriage today?

When I started talking to different writers about *Split*, the response was immediate and overwhelming. I was surprised at the initial enthusiasm—many said they'd always wanted an opportunity to write about their parents' divorce. They were eager to talk about it. It was a pivotal moment in their childhood. Some writers who didn't know me were at first hesitant to speak about such a personal topic, but before long were spilling their entire pasts. I soon discovered that most of these writers—whether white or people of color, male or female, raised on either a coast or in the great Midwest—listed being the product of a broken home as one of the single most important things they identified with.

The actual process of writing a personal essay, however, proved to be enormously difficult for everyone. While it was easy to identify with the subject, many soon realized that writing about their parents' divorce objectively was another matter. Old emotions arose. For some, the writing came out in an uncontrollable rush. Others were still angry and it seeped into their writing in odd, stilted ways. It wasn't uncommon to hear of authors writing through a blur of tears. And there were many worries. Did they have enough distance? Did they sound too whiney? Were they being fair to both parents? My role alternated between being an editor, a referee, and a sounding board for old grievances.

My own essay was written innumerable times, in different permutations. It was a struggle to write the story because I was so used to thinking of it as something that happened between the adults, something that happened *to* me. For a long time I did not feel like I had a proper handle on it—the work was either too angry or too sentimental, and would invariably wind up in the trash. I also worried over the repercussions of revealing family secrets that the adults sought to keep buried. I was scared to hurt my mother, who had chosen for so many years to remain silent about it. Would she refuse to talk to me? Would my grandmother ban me from the house?

Several writers expressed similar fears over upsetting their parents. Some never completed an essay because of it. For children of divorce, growing up meant living with the painful awareness that the family unit was a fragile structure; they were often left with the task of taking care of parents who seemed unable to take care of themselves, sometimes by protecting them or offering emotional support and guidance. Many of us still do this today. One woman recalls how her mother broke down crying on her shoulder after the divorce and said, "You are my rock." The writer was only ten years old at the time.

As I read the stories submitted for this anthology, I was struck by the realization that while most writers didn't know exactly why their parents had split, they could recall the moment it occurred quite clearly. Loud fighting behind a closed door. A long talk at the kitchen table. The sudden disappearance of a parent. Writer Alexandra Wolf's younger brother thought the sit-down talk they were ushered into meant he was getting a canoe. For them, as for many of us, the memory of the divorce is indelibly imprinted in our minds. As a kid, writer Jen Robinson likened it to a car crash in which she and her siblings were innocent bystanders only allowed to witness the divorce in its aftermath: no one to blame, just a messy collision, and everything changed.

In the pages that follow, you'll find a diverse group of stories that are as much essays about divorce as portraits of families on the brink of transition. Some recount the numerous times parents separated and got back together again before the final split; some chronicle the prolonged marriages that were kept together for the sake of the kids; still others write about how they had wished for years that their parents would divorce—only to experience extremely conflicted emotions when that wish was finally fulfilled.

Life after the divorce had its fair share of complications, and some explore the ups and downs of living in joint custody. One writer's wild teen years flourished in an atmosphere where parental authority broke down (Alexandra Wolf's "The Entropy Factor"). Another writer and her brothers were abducted across state lines. Almost all undertook the impossible task of trying to appease both parents, in addition to several stepparents, who were at times either resentful of or just plain baffled by their stepchild's presence.

Like millions of kids across the country, many learned to facilitate a wide and eclectic network composed of stepmoms and dads, half-brothers and -sisters, and stepgrandparents. The Brady Bunch experience it was not. Holidays were often stressful, as was the initial move into someone else's house. Some writers had to negotiate a series of stepfathers, stepmothers, and stepsiblings that came and went as their parents divorced and remarried. Kelly Murphy Mason writes heartbreak-ingly of the numerous stepmothers that entered her life after her own mother's death. Others were able to gain new friends and allies when the relationships stabilized—forging real bonds with their stepparents and stepsiblings.

Most kids of divorce accepted their situations unquestioningly, but not without carrying with them the knowledge that love could be sud-denly ripped apart. They cultivated a new belief in the impermanence of things, and the divorce became the lens through which they viewed themselves and the world. It was the lens through which all relationships would later be seen. One writer admits to being unable to fight with those he's intimately involved with; another didn't realize the divorce had affected him until he and his fiancée broke up. Some reflect on its impact on their own marriages and parenthood. One thing is startlingly clear: divorce is not an option. Writes Michelle Patient, "I cringe when I think about the havoc it would wreak on our now-one-year-old daughter's life."

There is a remarkable resiliency inherent in the essays, a resource-fulness that comes from growing up in a divorced household. There can be benefits to learning early on that one's parents are not perfect. Jen Robinson writes, "My early independence has made me confident I can handle more or less any situation. . . . I don't need to be rescued; I res-cue myself." And lessons in the fragility of relationships help them to better appreciate the ones that do work. "I can see how different my marriage is from my parents'," writes Amy Conway (pregnant with her first child at the time). "It's a true honest partnership."

When a divorced and happily remarried mother of a friend of mine first learned about this project, she asked, "Will it make already guilty-feeling parents feel even more guilty?" I was both surprised and appalled. (How self-centered our baby-boomer parents could be!) But her ques-tion keyed me into the larger issue of how differently parents and kids experienced the divorce and viewed its aftermath. Parents had dealt with the messy fall-out long ago, but still had leftover feelings of shame and guilt, which made them choose to remain silent about it, especially as they forged new relationships. Children, however, were left shell-shocked and voiceless.

Through writing, these fiction writers, poets, and essayists of diverse backgrounds have finally had the opportunity to tackle and make sense of the past. A number of them said that it was a healing and cathartic process. Working with each of them on their narratives and finally being able to write my own—no holds barred—has been an incredible learning experience for me. Hopefully, it will also be one for our readers.

The Early Years

NORMAL ABNORMAL

Jen Robinson

MY PARENTS WERE DIVORCED in 1978, when I was ten, my sister twelve. I grew up in a small Midwestern university town where my father was, and still is, a professor. My college-educated mother held a variety of jobs including children's librarian, stay-at-home mom, real estate agent, construction worker, and county auditor's assistant, eventually landing back in school for a master's degree in psychology (she's now semi-retired). Before the split, we lived in a pumpkin-colored house in a development of ranches and faux-colonials with street names like Onyx Court, Crystal Drive, Garnet Lane. The living room had gold shag wall-to-wall and a picture window that smelled of caulk. A sliding glass door in the dinette opened onto a redwood deck. At first there were no trees except the stump of a dead Dutch elm in the quarter-acre yard, but my parents planted fruit trees, a willow, a smokebush, lilacs, and pines. Later, my mother added flower and vegetable gardens, a raspberry patch, a grapevine. When I drove by a few years ago, it looked like the trees had always been there, but when I was a kid they were spindly things. There was one pine we called the Charlie Brown Christmas Tree because it was so scraggly it bent nearly double in a storm.

The way I remember it, we were happy—or maybe it's more accurate to say the question of whether we were or not had never crossed my mind: I was. What stands out from those years is roaming with my sister and a pack of other kids. The neighborhood wasn't far removed from cornfield, swampland, and riverbank, and we spent hours chasing frogs, climbing rocks, playing hide and seek. The swamp was the best: there were bullfrogs the size of kittens, and the lumpy, low-treed landscape provided endless secret places. In winter there were heavy snows (once there was a blizzard in April), and we'd make fantastic snow forts full of tunnels and ramparts. The city sprayed the double vacant lot next to our house with water after the first hard frost came every year to make an ice-skating rink; my dad loved to skate and was always ready to teach us his moves or lead a game of crack-the-whip. There'd be hot chocolate when we came in, and sometimes fried apples and popcorn. The biggest conflict I remember was ordinary sibling rivalry: who got to play Batman, whose turn it was to set the table, who was cheating at Monopoly.

Sounds almost too idyllic, doesn't it? Such is the power of language and memory. All those things are true; and there were also yearly trips to New York and Cape Cod, bikes for Christmas, reading aloud before bedtime. But in retrospect I see things I couldn't have been aware of as a child. The fact that a double lot in a new neighborhood stayed empty year after year, for example, now appears as an indicator of a depressed economy. The times must have seemed unstable, with unchecked inflation, Vietnam, Watergate. My parents, young and living on one income, must have been feeling financial and psychological stresses during the years of my childhood. Betty Friedan's *The Feminine Mystique* was written for my mother's generation, raised to value themselves as wives and mothers rather than individuals; my mother may have been suffering from a lack of that elusive quality, fulfillment. My father, in turn, may have been suffering from career worries as he sought to establish himself as a scholar. One or both of them must have retreated at some point from day-to-day communication. But how, why? I'll never know, since I was unaware, to say the least, of such adult concerns. What seems clear is that what was happy and safe from my perspective was for them a time of uncertainty, and, given the eventual outcome, growing dissatisfaction with each other. There's a dislocation between what I remember, that is, my reality, and what I now surmise to have been going on around me at the time, that is, their reality. I speculate that there is something important in the intrusion of their reality into mine at an age when I was still young enough to be thoroughly self-centered. Or is there some deeper psychological significance to my attaching to the predivorce period a kind of happy golden glow that perhaps isn't deserved by the actual facts? Would Freud have it that I'm still longing for a childhood that was ripped away from me? I don't find such questions useful; they smack of blame.

For many years I was unsure when exactly the divorce occurred. Though I know now that it was in 1978, the event retains a kind of haze in my memory. Was I ten? Eleven? It was early summer, but was it 1978 or 1979? I seem somehow to have lost a year. Paradoxically, while the exact year is slippery, the exact hour is sharply etched. In contrast to my parents, who both make a distinction between the time of palpable unhappiness, the time of separation, and the time of the final decree, for me there was a single epicenter in which their divorce occurred. This was the day my father left, the day they decided to divorce. The first unusual thing about that day was the closed door. I could hear Mom and Dad's voices rising and falling behind it as I lay with my feet up on the magenta-and-Lucite living room couch, a strictly forbidden act. I was reading Richard Scarry's *What Do People Do All Day*. I don't recall where my sister was. The idea that they might divorce fluttered into my mind, and I easily dismissed it. But when they came out, that was what was happening. My sister and I sat with my dad in the living room first. He told us that the divorce was between him and our mom, that it had nothing to do with us, that he was still our dad and loved us. Then we went to the master bedroom and sat with Mom. She said the same thing, that the divorce was between them, didn't have to do with us, and that they both loved us. When I asked her why they were getting divorced she said: "Because your father doesn't love me any more."

I believe her intention was to speak in terms a ten-year-old would understand, however, simplification can be misleading if it is not understood that it is simplification. I concluded that spontaneous cessation of love was the normal end to a relationship. As an adult, the evidence of my own feelings to the contrary hasn't always seemed sufficient contradiction: perhaps I'm not normal. Even now I haven't been able to completely rid myself of this fear. I tend to second-guess my decisions, still reacting to the idea that some one thing I say or do will create the expected rupture. Every act becomes freighted.

Sometime after the discussion with our parents, my dad started packing. My sister and I went across the street to tell a friend. This friend's parents often argued violently, and the three of us puzzled over how unlikely it was that her parents were not divorcing while ours were. We couldn't make sense of the apparent lack of connection between openness of anger and the actuality of who was splitting up. I don't recall ever seeing my parents argue. Ours was not a loud household, nor was it a household, then or after, in which problems were much discussed, at least not in the context of solving them; communication was buried. This is not to say I never saw them upset. My dad was given to an explosive "goddamn it!" when angry, but this struck me as funny more than anything else; my sister and I would imitate him as a joke, pointing our fingers and swearing. I didn't connect his outbursts with anything larger than momentary irritation. One day I walked into the kitchen and my father was hugging my mother, who was sobbing; this is the only time I remember noticing something seriously amiss between my parents. I didn't know how to understand it. They hadn't seen me come in, so I backed out quietly and never asked for an explanation. It was this that I pictured when my mother said, "Your father doesn't love me anymore."

After a while I went back over to our house, where I sat in the front yard and watched my dad going back and forth between house and car with boxes. I don't remember now if he said goodbye, though I think he must have; what sticks in my mind is watching him start the car, pull out of the driveway, disappear down the road. I can feel the prickle of summer-hot grass on my legs, and the sadness, which would have been there whether he said goodbye or not.

This is how I put it to myself then: the divorce was like a car accident I heard happen behind me and turned to look at. I couldn't say how it had happened or who might have been at fault, since I hadn't seen the cars moving toward each other; I could only describe how they looked after the collision. I convinced myself that I was an innocent bystander, merely observing, having nothing to do with the crash or its aftermath. It wasn't supposed to affect me; my parents were having a "good" divorce—still on speaking terms with each other, each still wanting to actively parent, Dad regular with alimony and Mom back to work. Everything was just fine.

OF COURSE THAT WASN'T QUITE TRUE. Dad wasn't there tying his tie in the bathroom mirror when I was brushing my teeth. Mom wasn't there when my sister and I came home from school. And when my parents were around, I now worried about both of them. My sister and I saw Dad on Sundays; he picked us up after lunch and brought us home after dinner.

His first apartment had a floor you felt you could lose your balance on and an unfinished feel—he hadn't taken much with him besides his clothes, a few pieces of furniture, the coffee pot. He didn't really know how to cook; we ate lots of chicken-fried steak and cabbage wedges. He was broken into twice. There was a time when he wanted to buy a house, but he didn't think he could afford one, so he considered a trailer. He was afraid, though, that if he lived in one I wouldn't visit him. I felt so guilty that I'd done anything to make him think that.

From overheard conversations, I knew my mother was worried about money and that this was the reason we were drinking powdered milk, which I hated. I knew also that she didn't like her job selling houses. Years later she still remembered this job with antipathy, writing to me that "in real estate I met people who spent all their time wallowing in bitterness." One night an older, well-dressed woman came to our house to interview my mother; I was already in bed when she came, but snuck out of bed to eavesdrop. From my position in the hallway I couldn't make out the words, but I could hear the distress in my mother's voice. I found out later that the woman was writing an article about divorce, but that night as I strained to listen in I was convinced that she was a psychiatrist who'd come to counsel my mother about how hard my selfishness was making her life.

At first, my mother would arrange not to be home when Dad picked us up and dropped us off, and I was glad. It was uncomfortable for me to be around them at the same time. I was a different person with each of them; each knew things about me the other didn't. I wanted to give each my undivided attention (obviously an impossible task when we were all together), and felt responsible for negotiating their interaction, since it was obvious that they would not have seen each other if they hadn't had to because of me and my sister. Things all of us had enjoyed together became sore spots. We were a musical family: my mother sang and played piano; my father played clarinet, recorder, and piano; my sister and I both played violin; and I had begun harp lessons the year before. We went to concerts; we listened to the Saturday afternoon radio broadcast of the Metropolitan Opera. Since the stereo and record collection were with my father now, my parents each made an attempt to provide my sister and me with one at home. My mother borrowed a turntable and speakers from friends. A few weeks later, my father bought a stereo system, which delighted us because it was made of a single sculpted piece of plastic. It had a cassette recorder set into the face, bright red knobs and levers, and a radio as well as a turntable and speakers. It didn't occur to us to mention the set Mom had borrowed. We came home excited, vying with each other to be the first to show Mom the new system's features. But she began to cry when she saw it. My poor parents! They were both trying so hard to be good to us, but they were so vulnerable. My mother needed comforting and reassurance; my father had to be kept from knowing that his well-intentioned purchase had precipitated such distress.

My sister and I became latchkey kids, our afternoons sprawling into fistfights, "Get Smart" reruns, messing around—almost never homework or practicing our instruments. We made agreements to cover for each other about practicing, which we did only on Wednesdays. Those nights, I'd make fried-egg sandwiches and wrap them up in tinfoil; when Mom came home, we'd be ready to pile in the car and eat on our way to violin lessons. Wednesday night was also church night, so after the lesson we'd get dropped off at the Unitarian Fellowship. I dreaded the violin lesson, because if my lack of practice became obvious I'd be in for a serious lecture later. The UU group, on the other hand, was fun: the other kids in the group were friends, and we'd do stuff like plan a weekend fast to raise money for families in El Salvador or just hang out and listen to music. When I was twelve or thirteen, after having begged for a pet for years, my mother found a dog for me: someone she knew was moving across the country and didn't want to bring their thirteen-year-old dog with them. My afternoons thereafter were mostly devoted to playing with Mandy, insofar as one can be said to play with a very old dog; but she was a wonderful animal, and I loved her.

THE CAR-ACCIDENT METAPHOR was a good one for a long time. It kept me from having to assign blame to either parent at a time when I felt responsible for and tenuously loved by both; it kept me from having to confront issues I didn't have the capacity to deal with. It was self-protective at a time when I needed to protect myself, and I'm proud of how resourceful I was at ten. As I grew to adulthood, however, it wasn't so useful—on one hand, I was reluctant to depart from its protection, which made me an observer rather than a participator in adult experience; on the other, I wasn't often able to wrestle the demons raised when I did take part. There were forays into blame in my teens. I once attacked my father at my grandfather's dinner table, accusing him of having had an affair; I argued incessantly with my mother, whose "Do you know how bad that makes me feel?" in response to my harshness still rings in my ears.

In my first year in college, I was delighted by the energy of New York City, by the discovery that I could enjoy schoolwork, and by the opportunity to go look at paintings whenever I wanted to. But I didn't make any friends I was interested in seeing again at the beginning of the second year (with the exception of one boy who'd already graduated, who became my boyfriend later that fall). In desperation, I crashed a party in a dorm room down the hall from mine, and was fortunate enough to meet some people who are now among my oldest friends. After that, I made friends easily; but always in distinct groups that seldom intersected. When they did, I felt internally pressured to please both groups and at the same time to negotiate the interaction between them (difficult when, say, the group that knew me as a party girl collided with the group that knew me as a quiet intellectual). Occasionally such situations would become unbearable, and I'd end up making one set of friends both mystified and angry by ignoring them altogether. I realized at some point that I needed to reintegrate myself, to let myself be the whole of who I was with everyone who knew me.

I'd have to take the risk of saying what I wanted, and in order to do that, I'd have to know what I wanted. That was never a problem when I was alone; but when I was with other people I'd lose track because I was trying so hard to figure out what I should want. When I did know what I wanted, moreover, I had a hard time figuring out when to say so. I'd often pick wrongly—backing down when I should have stood my ground, getting pissed when I should have let it go. A separate but related problem was that I didn't have any idea how to get what I wanted; the gulf between wanting and having often seemed unbridgeable. One solution to these difficulties was to be alone a lot. I traveled by myself for four months when I was twenty-two; to some of my friends, that seemed brave, but to me it was far easier than having to tell someone else what I wanted.

That task is still difficult, though I'm no longer caught between my parents: they are who they are, I am who I am. But the act of tracing present circumstances to past events is complicated by the fact that I'm probably in the worst position to distinguish what in me comes from external events and what from the personality I was born with. Put another way, what is generalizable about the effects of divorce, and what is unique to me? It's impossible to know, and uncertainty spirals into obstruction. My parents, after all, did have a good divorce by comparison to many. The economic hardships my mother faced after the divorce, though not trivial (at one point she considered applying for food stamps), never became disastrous. Post-divorce relations between my parents were strained but never descended into acrimony. I know they both did what they thought best, and I love and respect them for it. From many valid points of view, then, I don't have anything to complain about, and on some level I can't help fearing that you'll read me as just plain neurotic. I begin to worry that what I've written concentrates too much the negative side of the coin without acknowledging the positive. My early independence, for example, has made me confident I can handle more or less any situation. I've been able to translate doing things on my own into getting things on my own, which hasn't been easy but has been personally rewarding. I don't need to be rescued; I rescue myself.

I'VE BEEN USING THE WORD *parents* thus far to mean my mother and father; however, when I was in high school two more people were added to the definition, becoming the four I now refer to collectively as my parents. In the beginning, this was convenient shorthand, less complicated (and less inviting to personal questions) than "my mother and stepfather" or "my father and the woman-he-lives-with-who-I-think-of-as-my-stepmother." But I really do have four parents: there are four people in my life that have helped shape it, though not always in ways one might expect. Theoretically, I might have gained a multiplicity of relationship models from the stable, long-term relationships both parents have been in since my teens. That wasn't the case, though I did gain other things that became important to me as an adult. This is perhaps the most difficult part of my experience to write about; the interactions are complex, and examining the combustion between my mother and myself during my teens is fraught with still unresolved danger.

My mother met my stepfather when I was fourteen, and they were married two years later, in the summer of 1984. He had three sons from his first marriage, of whom he had custody; his ex-wife, like my dad, still lived in town. An addition was built onto my stepdad's house, and after the wedding, we moved in. My sister and oldest stepbrother, about a month apart in age, left for college a few months later. The second stepbrother was just three days younger than I was; we began junior year at the same high school that fall. (I remember sitting next to him in the library one day in ninth grade, not saying anything but observing him surreptitiously and thinking, that's the boy whose father is sleeping with my mother.) My youngest stepbrother was two years behind. During the first year of the new marriage, my mother encouraged me to treat my stepbrothers as if we had always been siblings, and asked me to treat my stepfather in a similar manner. She wanted us to be a real family—but what is real? What is family? At this distance I can both admire the energy my mother devoted to reconstructing a family and acknowledge that the process was at best uncomfortable for me. With, I suppose, typical teen angst, I felt I was being asked to participate in a lie. I didn't see us as a family; I saw us as a bunch of strangers who lived together. Moreover, in the five years since the divorce I'd become accustomed to feeling an "adult" responsibility. I chafed at returning to a child role. I resisted for all kinds of reasons, not the least of which was that fact that she was my mom—and there were few parts of our relationship by then that were not bound up in the coil of push-me pull-you. The kid who'd been so afraid of making her mother's life difficult turned into a teen who did make her mother's life difficult.

The similarity in age between me and my steps prompted endless, and for us, distressing, references to "The Brady Bunch." There simply wasn't time in the two years between my mother's remarriage and my departure for college for my steps and me to forge relationships, particularly since we were all teenagers, insecure and hormonally wired. That first year we mostly ignored each other. At the end of the year, we went on a family vacation. I felt coerced; I didn't want to go, and in response was sulky and rude throughout the two weeks of driving cross-country. The next-to-last day of the trip, visiting relatives of my stepdad's that none of us except him had ever met before, things boiled over between my stepbrothers and me. Temporarily left alone in the living room, the three of us (my sister and older stepbrother weren't there) began by sniping and ended by yelling. On their side, it was "We never asked for you to come live in our house and we don't want you there!" On my side it was, "I never asked to go live in your house! I don't want to be there!"

We didn't really start to connect until my middle stepbrother and I had left home. Fall 1986 was the first semester of our freshman year in college, and we both flew home from New York for Thanksgiving. At the table, my mother sat next to my stepdad; next to him sat my father and stepmother. Then came my stepfather's ex-wife (my stepbrothers' mother) and her partner. My stepbrothers and I were on the opposite side, and rounding out the table were my father's father and brother. (My older sister and stepbrother had not come home). My stepbrothers and I sat in uncomfortable silence, listening to the adults drop stones into a chasm of stilted conversation. We excused ourselves as soon as possible, and for the first time, instead of retreating separately (as we'd done in the past) went together to the basement. Someone started a game of pool. I don't remember exactly what we said, but it became clear that we shared an opinion about what was going on upstairs.

The following summer the three of us lived at home for the last time. I took Psych 101 and waitressed for the University's catering outfit, which meant I left the house in the morning and got back late in the evening. My middle stepbrother, meanwhile, had a job baking at the town's new bagel shop, so he worked overnight, getting home around five or six in the morning. I'd get up when he returned; neither of our parents would be awake yet, and we'd sit in the driveway smoking pot until I left and he went to sleep. When I got back at night, he'd be waking up, and we'd do the same thing until he went to work and I went to sleep. On the Fourth of July, he broke up with the girl he'd been dating since high school (he'd come home for the summer to be with her), and I went on a date with a guy from work who'd been asking me all summer. He took me to a kegger where I didn't know anyone and I got so drunk that for the first and only time I blacked out; I came to at home with my head over the toilet. My brother and I spent the rest of the night hanging out in the basement commiserating.

My father met my stepmother the same year my mother remarried, and they began living together shortly thereafter. The summer after I graduated from high school my father and "stepmother" (they didn't marry until I was nearly thirty) left town for a month and a half, and hired me to take care of their house while they were away. This included paying bills (they left blank checks and stamps), watering plants, and repainting the garage. In return, I was paid $200 (a huge sum for me at the time) and had free access to their house, a stuccoed 1920s bungalow my dad had bought some years previously. I began the garage project imagining myself a heroic wage-earner toiling ceaselessly to fulfill the responsibility entrusted to me, but soon realized that standing on a rickety ladder scraping rotten paint off the shadeless side of an old shed is hot, dirty, and boring. I began breaking for iced tea more and more often; the day I brought a book with me, it was all over. The month and a half I'd had to complete the project telescoped to three days, and the garage still wasn't fully scraped, let alone primed. I spent those last three days solid on that ladder, sweating more than ever. By the time they returned, the job at least looked done. The paint must have started peeling again in short order, but they never said a word. They paid me and praised me as if I'd done the job right, which, intentionally or not, was a more effective punishment than a thousand recriminations.

For the most part, though, I was never in doubt as to how my stepmother felt and why, whether she was angry or amused or proud. If she was angry, it was because I'd acted thoughtlessly, as when I left the bathmat damply balled on the floor; she made it clear that I had been inconsiderate to the next person in, who'd have to do what I hadn't. She made me think about how my behavior might affect other people, and I'm grateful to her for that. Conversely, if she was interested or amused by something I said, I knew the response was genuine. Because I wasn't in the dark about where I stood with her, I trusted her opinion of my behavior, and I wanted that opinion to be good. She was tough; I couldn't get away with a lot of stuff that worked with my mother and father, because she expected me to be an adult, not a snotty teen. I made a concentrated effort to rise to her expectation, and I learned a lot about how to be a responsible adult from her. I'm still learning from her example; she lives life more fully and with more integrity than anyone else I know.

THE STORY OF AMELIA EARHART terrified me in sixth grade.

"You mean no one knows what happened to her? And no one's ever going to know?" I've always been a knowledge collector; I want to know everything about everything. I majored in history in college because reading all about the past was a better story to me than any work of fiction. The intricate contingency of who-what-when acted in combination with the variously interpreted whys to enthrall me. I get excited about something and want to know all about it; I remember obscure details; I think everything is important. When I was a senior in college, I wrote a paper on the Iran-Contra scandal. I'd read Hannah Arendt's *Crises of the Republic*, and I was trying, with more enthusiasm than perspicacity, to emulate her style of analysis. Rereading the paper recently, I realized that what interested me then was not so much the events themselves (though they are both fascinating and appalling) as the process by which the ability to know becomes subverted. My paper mentioned only briefly the actual facts (the horrendous death toll in Nicaragua, for example), which the Iran-Contra conspirators' lies obscured, concentrating instead on the Byzantine structure of who lied to whom when for what putative purpose. I wanted to know how we know things; I wanted to know whether we know things at all.

These kinds of questions still rank at the top of my list, and I link this fascination with epistemology to my parents' divorce. The divorce came out of the blue. I was aware of a troubling, mysterious tension between my parents, and I had friends whose parents were divorced, so I wasn't living inside a bubble. But experience is often contradictory; one can be aware and innocent at the same time, especially in childhood. When I'd asked myself as I lay on the living room couch that day, "What if Mom and Dad get divorced?" it was like asking, "What if I'd been born in ancient Greece?" It wasn't any kind of reality. As I grew older, that reality remained mysterious. Since I'd been too young during the years of their marriage to be aware of, or indeed interested in, my parents as separate individuals with their own relationship, I had no meaningful memories of their relationship with which to interpret the past. Knowledge appeared inaccessible. What strikes me now about the car accident analogy is that it assumes there was something to be known. And further, that there was some reason I should know it. Why didn't I know it? Why couldn't I know it? As a teenager and young adult, there seemed to be something everyone else knew that was just out of my reach. In my midtwenties I made up the mantra "There are no rules besides the ones you create for yourself," in order to combat the sense that if only I, too, had possession of the magic playbook everyone else seemed to take for granted, I'd be able to have the life I wanted. I became cautious in new situations, looking for the new set of rules that might apply.

This suggests a final problem with the car accident analogy. It not only assumes there is something to be known, it asserts that the thing can't be known. When I began to think about writing about my parents' divorce, it seemed to me that in terms of the analogy, it couldn't be known because the observer is passive. And it was no longer tenable for me to visualize myself as a passive observer of my own life; I needed to be active, and to realize that the thing to be known is neither objective nor concrete. So I decided to interview my family members. In doing so, I wanted to reconstruct the past in order to reimagine it. I wanted to convince myself that the theories I'd built around the concurrent absence and presence of knowledge were never true, that I could restructure my very feelings. I wanted to be an active doer as well as a passive knower, to organize myself not around some Thing, there, to be known or unknown, but around self-created understanding. I didn't want to be doomed to fail in some way I couldn't comprehend and remain in a state of longing.

The interviews with my parents revealed that neither of them fully understood, then or now, what caused their relationship to dissolve. This now seems unremarkable: who can really understand all the complexities of human interaction? And if we could, wouldn't life be pretty boring? In my parents' case, it turns out there wasn't anything to know beyond the ordinary (albeit painful) details of a man and woman falling out of sync, not communicating, not knowing how to find their way back—and so becoming irretrievably unhappy with each other. Yet the effect on my life doesn't strike me as mundane at all. Initially, this was contradictory and disappointing (I'd convinced myself that what I sought was not answers but greater understanding, but I confess I'd expected my unknowns to suddenly resonate with sense). But the knot untangles: my reality isn't theirs. I already knew what they told me; I'd always known it.

THE EXPERIENCE OF WANTING to know, though, has been deeply important to me in as many wonderful ways as hampering ones. The drive to know things and the prospect of all the things there are to be known is what makes life worth living for me. It's the complexity of human experience, the simultaneous desire and inability to know, which energizes my own work as a poet. I've been writing since I was a kid (the first writing I remember was a play about lion poachers, heavily influenced by *Born Free*, when I was about six), and I became increasingly interested in poetry in the early 1990s, during a period when I was ending both a long-term relationship and an attempt to make a career in the film industry. I wasn't a particularly good art department assistant. I was competing with people who'd been to art school and knew a lot more than I did about fabrication and design, and though I was eager to learn, I was behind the curve and unsure of my ability. I had various day jobs in the wholesale antique business (my first job after college had been in an auction house) while I tried to earn my chops working on student films and deferred-payment projects. I was broke and tired most of the time. I sometimes think, though, that if I weren't a failed set decorator I wouldn't be a poet at all; as my interest in becoming an art director flagged, my energy was redirected toward writing. It took some time to

realize that what I was doing was making poems. When I began thinking of my writing that way, the process became exciting. Since I didn't
have a lot of money (one year I made $12,000, which in retrospect I'm
impressed I lived on, though it was miserable at the time), I'd go to the
new Barnes & Noble that had armchairs and read Gerard Manley Hopkins, HD, Rilke. I didn't go to the library because it was worse to take a
book home and then have to give it back than it was to not take it home
at all. I played with syllabic forms in my head on the subway to and from
work. And I began looking for venues to go hear contemporary poets'
work. Coincidentally, poetry was enjoying a revival in the public eye,
energized by the spoken word performance scene. I'd heard about a
place called the Nuyorican Poets Café, and after a few weeks of walking around the Lower East Side after work I found it. Soon I was reading my work in the open mike session after the Friday night poetry slam,
as well as meeting and sharing work with other poets. Eventually I was
one of the slam performers myself, and started my own open mike night
at a bar in Brooklyn where I sometimes worked.

One day a friend living overseas asked me to send her some of my
work. As I typed it up on the computer, it occurred to me that with some
formatting changes I could make a kind of booklet; from there it was a
small step to printing multiple copies. I put a graphic on the front cover
and a made-up press name on the back cover and started handing them
out at readings, trading for zines and chapbooks. Through this kind of
distribution, my poems landed on the desk of an independent press pub-
lisher, who called to ask if I wanted to do a book with him. Needless to
say, I did! That was in 1995, and I've been busy since then; I now perform my work regularly around the country, submit to and am published
in journals and magazines, and do freelance editing and writing.

I value curiosity and imagination—the life of the mind—above all
else. I'm incredibly lucky to have some ability to translate my inner world
to others, and to live in circumstances that enable me to exercise that
ability. The violin lessons paid off, too: the early training in pitch and
memorization have given me a better ear and a capacity for remembering details that I wouldn't otherwise have. These things are immensely

valuable in the practice of writing, no doubt contributing to my attraction to writing in the first place. They also make my day-to-day experiences richer, from enjoying Tito Puente while I make my coffee in the morning to doing crossword puzzles.

I enjoy doing crosswords so much, in fact, that a couple of years ago I decided to see if I could figure out how to make one. I was freelancing in an office at the time, and I tested out my first puzzles on my coworkers, who were all avid puzzlers. Some time later, a friend who publishes an avant-garde literary magazine asked me to make one for his publication, further suggesting that I make it as difficult to do as possible. I followed his suggestion and discovered a new kind of thing altogether; as puzzle editor for the magazine, I make crosswords that can be both worked as a puzzle and read as a poem, treading a line between analysis and intuition. I think this is a good metaphor for where I am now. All the things I think I've dealt with are still waiting in my pockets to bite me if I forget about them; every clarity seems ephemeral. But I have a life that makes me happy. If there are difficulties and contradictions, so be it—maybe that's what it's all about.

CALIFORNIA OVERBOARD

Paula Gilovich

Seattle, Washington, 2001: Recalling My Parents' Divorce

When I was six weeks old, my dad walked out during a diaper change. Three days later, while my mother was changing my diapers, he returned. In third grade, he left again. Then in sixth grade, then eighth; finally, after my freshman year of high school, my parents officially, legally divorced.

To communicate to us clearly that this split was final—this was no longer a test—my mother took my sister, Andrea, and me on a Mexican divorce vacation. We ventured to Cabo San Lucas in the middle of August. There, we were to discuss our new union—just us girls. But it was simply too hot to discuss anything. The swimming pool served to cook rather than cool, and a mere five minutes under Mexican sun left our California skin painfully burnt. So we spent day after day riding twenty minutes into town to shop at three tiny stores.

On the road into town, I watched the oily horizon shimmy under the heat as we sped toward it in a rickety cab. The blurry horizon declared to me that the future was uncertain.

Sure enough, a couple of years later, Andrea and I came home from school (we had just learned that the balance of *A*s to *C*s were actually in our favor—something that had not happened since the divorce) to discover my mother and father together at the kitchen table sipping hot coffee. The scene was uncanny. The mugs the two of them held were unrecognizable; neither of them ever drank coffee, separately or together. More importantly, coffee suggests niceties and neither had spoken one kind word to or about the other since long before they divorced.

Andrea and I exhaled the strangeness of the scene, and then inhaled all that was far too familiar. We knew before they could put their coffee down that our parents were getting back together again.

As quickly and nonchalantly as they announced their reunion, the two of them revealed that they weren't going to live together this time around. My father was to keep his apartment, and we would remain at the house. I remember thinking, yeah, that's right, admit *something* here in this disingenuous moment.

All of my California friends with their California parents and their California divorces dreamed of their parents getting back together. They dreamed of reconciliation on the eve of adulthood. They had infantile habits that seemed to accompany their fairytale cravings: still wetting beds at twelve, sucking thumbs at sixteen, unable to sleep with the lights off even after graduation.

Wanting my parents to reconcile was admitting that I wanted the two of them to divorce again. I couldn't do it. And so, at the kitchen table, in the spirit of togetherness, I couldn't help but wish that one of the large, low-flying 747s that disrupted our TV's reception daily, might choose that moment to crash land on our house while we all stood there gathered as a family.

The Salon, San Jose, California, Right Off Race Street, February 2000

Francesca's false eyelash on her right eye keeps falling off. My mother, in a rush and high heels, scuffles back and reassures Francesca, "Okay, okay, I got it this time." My mother adds another line of glue and then uses her long fingernails to straighten the eyelash. "Close your eye so I don't glue this spider right to your eyeball," she says tersely. In one slowed-down moment in a frenzied transsexual hair salon, my mother places eyelash to eye like a diamond to the center of a gold band. A hundred men in various stages of redressing themselves as women crowd Carla's, the tranny salon. They're all preparing for the Transsexual Cotillion Ball 2000 in San Francisco that night. My mother invited me to come along, insisting that it would be a blast. She uses language like this, she wears platform flip-flops, and she professionally turns men into women, one evening at a time. She's always been youthful, but she hasn't always been a transsexual hairstylist and make-up artist. No, her career has taken this shift in the absence of my father.

Through the chaos of the salon, my mother asks me if my father ever called me on Christmas. "No," I answer. "But I didn't call him either." Her back-combing becomes more vigorous. "Well, he can just forget about you two," she says, referring to my sister and me, "because now he has two *new* babies. They're both boys, right?"

It's true. My dad is seventy-two years old and he has two baby boys. She knows this.

"I hear he's fat now," states Francesca, as if she has ever once met my father. Franny is the support my mother has always needed. Nothing is more validating than a man who no longer wants to be a man telling a 100 percent man-hater like my mother that men are no good.

"*Mom*," I say.

My petite mother—size one, maybe two—is a high femme fatale with a strong sexuality and a fierce talent for cynicism. She's got eyes like Ms. Taylor's and skin like a thirty-eight-year-old. Since the final divorce from my father, she's been known to say, "If I ever get a fatal disease, I'm putting a bullet in your father's head—I'm serious." She may well be serious, but she usually cracks herself up into tears after giving such a bold declaration.

Perched on the only empty stool, watching as the trans women race past me in femininity, both figuratively and quite literally, I realize then how my mother will only contend with a man these days if he agrees to wear a dress.

Dad, All My Life

My father is the charismatic center of the New World for me. I bear his full name, only slightly feminized and thus, I've been reminded most of my life that I bear many of his more difficult attributes.

Paul is a storyteller of high fortune, mad success, and brilliant outcomes. His stories start as ants and quickly morph into skyscrapers. His world seems like a stiff drink—optimistic relief with a bitter aftertaste.

Paul looks like a cross between Ronald Reagan and Johnny Cash. Like Johnny Cash, he wears all black, mostly, and when he's not smiling he seems to loom, a dark man with wild black eyebrows that appear to be glued on in a permanent frown. Born in 1930, he grew up rough, the son of Yugoslavian immigrants; when he was two his father died of black lung disease. But he's also a son of the Golden State, a purebred California dreamer, and it's this sun-drenched composure that reminds me of Reagan: his speech patterns, his smiling eyes, his steel-toed optimism, the way his age wears like leather on his California face.

Paul is often heard saying: "Oil and water. Your mother and I are like oil and water. We just don't mix."

He's got all sorts of old-timey sayings. When we wanted something—a piece of candy, or a new toy—he'd say, "Wish in one hand and spit in the other, see which one gets full first," and then laugh and laugh. Every time.

Paul has the ability to electrify the room—anyone's body in the room—with the purest form of optimism. Oftentimes he would secretly declare me the smartest of his children, fully confident that I would go on to do fantastic, brilliant things. (Paul had three boys from a previous marriage and as adults, we uncovered identical stories of being appointed the smartest kid.)

But as I tried to set myself on a path for brilliance, I couldn't conceive of a suitable career or triumph that would match his enthusiasm; I took an inventory of the universe, and realized no, nothing would really work, not a doctor, not an astronaut, not the president.

Paul has the ability to electrocute his setting and then the whole world burns down under his rage. I was six when I first understood that nothing could gain amnesty from his pungent disdain. My father had intense anger not only for his living, breathing family, but also for the small inanimate objects that often live quietly and without harm in other people's homes. On this poignant, memorized afternoon, a Sunday newspaper turned up missing and the family watched from the bamboo bar in the family room as Paul, in the living room, jumped up and down on his $500 leather briefcase until the frame poked through and the briefcase was no longer a briefcase. The newspaper was supposed to be inside the briefcase, and since it was not, the briefcase was convicted and sentenced to death.

Almaden Valley, 1982, Guessing It's April, the Cruelest Month

My mother wakes me close to midnight. For a ten-year-old midnight is, indeed, the middle of the night, and in the child's imagination it is waking to find oneself in the dark desert of adulthood. Still in my pajamas, she zips a sweatshirt over me and asks me if I will go on a drive with her. I don't bring up the subject of Andrea, because this moment, somehow, is intended just for Mom and me. Generally, Andrea and my mother are closer, as I resemble my father so completely—this is what I've been told.

On the cold leather seats of the white Cadillac, I practice locking and unlocking the doors electrically. I can get a beat going if I really concentrate. When my mother's anxiety is not soothed by my compulsion, and she threatens to ground me into eternity, I stop and look out onto the empty road. When one of those large, six-lane suburban roads turns up deserted, it's shocking. I couldn't imagine the Mississippi being any wider than Saratoga Avenue in San Jose, California.

Jeannie, my mother, is silent. When the thick tangle of freeway appears, looming like a single mountain, and we appear to be heading toward it, I know exactly where we're going. We're going to Cory Hunter's house. Cory is my sister's best friend. In our small experimental private school, Cory is in Andrea's class. Dylan, her older brother, is in my class, and he's what my friends and I refer to—for alliterative purposes—as "The Dick."

For a time there, when Diane, Cory's mother, was still married to her husband, and Cory and Andrea were best friends (both little tan kids who liked to pretend they were frogs), everything was fantastic. My mother and Diane forged a relationship over driving and picking up the kids and the gross organization and time that took—but also, as ladies, they got their nails manicured together. The Hunters with their two kids, my parents with theirs, these adults were suspended for a time in that California suburban life that seems to occur perpetually at dusk—everything is chilled Chardonnay, sliding glass doors, swimming pools, and hot tubs.

In the distant future, my mother will fall in love with the toppled clichés, as they signify her heroism. After a sip of red wine, held by her elegant, unaging hands, she will note with great disdain and comic sass that Diane had the worst taste imaginable—although thin, Diane wore polyester pants with elastic waistbands; also, Diane never used toner on her self-bleached hair.

My mother recalls, too, helping Diane a great deal when her husband walked out on her. She recalls insisting that my father be kind to Diane during the hard transition of divorce, and suggesting that Diane become the new secretary at my dad's start-up computer company.

We arrive in Almaden Valley, a development community made of particle board. Taste is nowhere here among bleached pavement driveways, kidney-shaped lawns, and the dawn of plastic mailboxes. My mother takes the Cadillac in a memorized direction, turning left, then softly right.

We arrive at the Hunters' cul-de-sac. She turns the key and we hear the small electrical death of the engine.

There we sit around the corner from the Hunters', not yet able to see the house. Then my mother, half-choking, asks if I will peek around the corner. I heave the heavy door open and walk barefoot onto someone's lawn. Before me is my father's 1967 Cougar, parked for the night in the Hunters' driveway. The light is still on in the living room.

All I can think of is how I'm gonna kick Dylan Hunter's ass when I get to school tomorrow.

Notification at a Carl's Jr. Restaurant, Stevens Creek Road, San Jose, California, 1980

On my dad's first day back in San Jose after a month-long Asian business trip, he takes me, alone, out to a Carl's Jr. restaurant. When we get there, I'm surprised and a little humiliated to find that I'm the only one eating.

A plastic brown tray heaped with zigzag french fries arrives at our table and our table marker (number 34) is swiped away. I reach across the fries to grab a ketchup packet, but I can't open it. I just squish it in my fingers. My father says, "Now I want to tell you something, but I don't want you to jump to conclusions. I wanted to tell you and Andrea separately because you're very different people. Andrea is like your mother—she needs a lot of time and energy to adjust to new situations. You're a lot like your dad. Tough."

He socks me in the arm. My father's eyes disappear with a smile. He's full-blooded Croatian, but he looks very Korean. He's real tall at six-three with small black eyes and beautifully pale olive skin. His hair is a glistening black. "And you've got a temper like your dad," he adds. At this, he's laughing.

He doesn't have to go any further. What is understood thoroughly by children is discussed at such length by parents. But of course he does, explaining where he's going to live, how often he will see us, how we won't be yanked out of private school. It does mean we won't go to Disneyland together this year, not as a family—but that for sure someone will take us.

"Whether it's me or your mother," he says as he borrows a sip of my milkshake, an obvious gesture of relief.

Money, Silicon Valley, and 1986

More than an indisputable love, my father wanted an indisputable amount of money. In those days, the word to describe his electric desire was "multimillionaire." Even when we were little girls, he would detail his grand, big-money plans. We filled penny rolls, me in a Garfield nightgown, my sister suited up in Smurfs, as he told us how short the path was between him and fabulous success. This was the sign we were to look for: If he ever really made it, he would arrive home that evening in a DeLorean or a Porsche 920. He loved the DeLorean best, but it only came in silver. If we saw him in this car, we were to instantly pack our rooms into suitcases—no, not even pack, just clamber into the back seat—and catch a ride to our new house, which would already be furnished with rooms full of toys still in their packages.

To tide him over until the day he could fling open the DeLorean's winged door and speed into the sunset on Highway 280, Paul bought himself a T-top Trans Am, red, with the license plate "BIRDBOY." He bought it from an ex-pat Brit who had headed out of town after gambling and losing a fortune in the computer business.

Even if my father was not a "multimillionaire," for some time we had a considerable amount of money. I remember asking my mother for money to go to the mall. She slid one of the crisp hundred-dollar bills from her wallet and into my hand. From her waterbed, she said, "Now, I want you to at least get one sweater out of this. Don't be lame." In the eighties, my mother loved the word *lame*.

My father had instituted the ideology of big spending in our family. Sick with the Silicon Valley fever, he mimicked those men whose companies were indeed going public and making them rich, those men who had mortgaged their houses and crossed their fingers—who now were able to laugh in relief and pay the house off and sell it in one day.

So I might be taken out of school to catch a sale at the Esprit outlet in San Francisco, where I could watch the pile of clothes at the register and the bill climb digitally past $700. And I was surprised in second-period math by a message from the principal's office that my mother would be picking me up in a moment—because, it turned out, my father had gotten the company plane for the day and we were going to Disneyland. Each November, I was taken out of school again, so we could fly to Puerto Vallarta and occupy our tropical time-share for a month. All of these trips culminated in penthouse suites atop high-rise hotels, with views that made us sick, living rooms we never sat in and kitchens we never cooked in. My father always dared me to swallow one of the oysters on the half-shell that shimmered on the ivory plate resting on the umbrella table next to the heated swimming pool. There was champagne in the refrigerator every time I opened it.

For this, my father mortgaged the house three times over.

The Day After, 1984–1990

During the cold war of my youth, I saw a school-sponsored film called *The Day After*. Do you remember *The Day After*? Explosions knocking bodies through the air, wildfire and gas explosions sucking the oxygen from the atmosphere—all encompassed in that supersonic mushroom cloud.

Reagan was president, and the fear of nuclear war began to mount, and I got confused in my terror and anxiety. Nuclear war, divorce— nuclear family divorce war? All of my friends talked about nuclear war, fascinated by the endless carnage, a planet of innocent bystanders; as we talked, every last one of my friends' parents divorced. *The Day After* seemed to last from 1984 to 1990, to encompass all the red anger and blue dread in our hearts.

So the children of the eighties, at least, were braced for an explosion. My father, a staunch Reagan Republican, didn't heed the warning signs. His company went belly-up, as they say, in a day. Moments later, it seemed, my family lost $750,000 on Black Monday. To begin repaying his sudden huge debts, the home my father had designed—our family home since 1970—had to be sold immediately.

Years later, in the lingering half-life of our family's disaster, my mother shows me documents of stock purchases, patents, and lawsuits. We sit on the deck of her apartment and somehow, with all the papers laid out under the sun, all those frozen disasters exposed, we can both feel pity for my father. "He was a fool with money," she sighs, "and I was a fool to believe him. I remember one evening we were out to dinner, his favorite activity. We must have spent a million dollars on Chinese food back then. This young kid was pitching his great new idea about hard drives or whatever and Paul, within five minutes of the pitch, said with enthusiasm that he would invest a great deal of money. He loved saying 'Yes' to the deal, because he loved being asked."

My mother crosses her legs and bounces her bare foot. The anxiety of this particular past will always create a contagious series of twitches. I start rolling the ashtray edgewise on the glass table. She continues even through the noise I make. "This kid who wanted very much for your father to invest started to get nervous. He felt like Paul was being too hasty and asked him to wait to commit so much. I couldn't believe it. We were all sitting there pleading with him to slow down. But it just furthered the battle of egos."

Ironically, if my father had had the savvy just to keep our family home—a home that had cost $40,000 to build—until today, he would have been a millionaire.

The New Condo, Hacienda Street, Campbell, California, 1990

Andrea screams, "Stop it!" But I don't. I run around our new condo, our never-before-lived-in condo, following the circular layout, opening all of the cabinet doors. (I'm legally an adult, but it is a strain for me to act as such.) My sister has developed an aversion to open cabinets and open doorways—she compulsively shuts them. To this day, she considers it nauseating to see anything ajar.

I continue opening the cabinets and now drawers as she runs behind me and closes each one.

After we sold the house and my parents were back together, we all needed to decide where to live. My dad took an apartment, in keeping with their promise that we wouldn't all live together ever again. And somehow, from his ruined credit, he was able to summon a fancy condominium for us. Andrea and I both had French doors looking out onto a balcony. There was a hot tub in the backyard, and my mother had a Jacuzzi in her master bathroom. Do not get me wrong, however, such a living situation—that we were not in a house in the Saratoga hills any longer—meant there was always a ghostly presence of shame.

My mother is filing her nails, sitting at the bar. This image is strangely sad, because I have never before in our history seen my mother filing her own nails. Without looking up, she says, "You two need to stop running around, you're making the dog crazy." We were; Neko, our little Spitz, was running around the feet of my mother's bar stool, absorbing our mad energy.

The phone rings. My father is in Singapore and we have been waiting for his call.

My mother answers. When we realize her head is hung low and she's beginning to tear up, we both stop the chase. Andrea and I stand in the kitchen.

"Paul. No. No way. You are not doing this to me again."

Paul has called from Singapore to tell my mother they need to split again—this time for good—because he wants to marry someone else. This woman he met in a Singapore bar. The affair had spanned the trip before this trip, but finalized—meaning my father had already asked her to marry him—during this trip. I can picture my father just getting up the guts to call and rest his conscience right then. Thinking he was being responsible, I'm sure, for calling Jeannie from abroad, instead of waiting to get back to break the news.

Like most accidents, it all happened so quickly. I *knew* this was going to happen again. I had pledged to be prepared, like I recently pledged to be prepared for the next earthquake (we had just had a 7.2), but I had forgotten what you are supposed to do in the case of your parents splitting permanently again for the fourth time—stand in the door frame?

I was instantly sick. I had a fever and my nose started running. Andrea snuck quietly away and went upstairs. She didn't come out of her locked room until the next day.

Lost Condo/New Marriage, Three Months Later

In the era of lost condo/new marriage, there does not seem to be a port of entry to the memory of that time. Exactly one fragment remains.

Andrea and I both remember standing by the swimming pool at his shabby apartment complex. I was nineteen and about to do laps in a bikini, Andrea was doing somersaults in the pool and our father stood over us in his black jeans and his black boots, his skin an odd color simply because it lacked all color. We had written him a letter explaining quite nicely why we never, ever wanted to meet his new wife. She was going to arrive in three days.

As he started to kick over the lounge chairs and generally cause a scene, speaking of all the money he had invested in us over the years and how we owed him—I jumped in the pool and committed to staying underwater. It is the equivalent of covering one's ears, I guess. Andrea swam into the shallow end and stayed under the surface there. I swam to the deepest point and put my palm flat on the drain, so I could feel it pull at me.

We both knew our father's fear of water would stop him from coming after us.

My mother remembers a deep end of a different kind. A couple months prior, Paul had had her sign a bunch of papers that supposedly signed the condominium over to her; the idea was that if anything happened to him, she would own it and creditors would not come after her. They had never legally married again, so this would work. But in the event that he left her, she would be saddled with huge monthly payments she could not make. When he did make that phone call from Singapore, she remembers profoundly, frantically understanding just how he had screwed her. She tore through piles of bills and papers, creating a disaster area and in that pile, she discovered he hadn't paid on the condo in months. Days later, she received notice of impending foreclosure.

The New Kids, Seattle, Washington: March 1997

My father calls me from Colorado to tell me he's picked a name out for his not-yet-born son or daughter.

"If it is a boy, I'm going to name it Paul. If it's a girl, her name will be Paulina. What do you think?"

I'm pretty shocked. "What? Are you serious? What about me?"

"I'm not naming him or her *Paula*. That name is all yours."

This is the same guy who didn't get himself a new wedding band for his new marriage. Instead, he had the exact same ring he gave my mother refashioned for his new wife.

On Return to California, Descending on Silicon Valley, 2001

From the point of descent, California appears terminally ill. The yellow sky turns to a gray-brown smudge that does not blur the horizon, but obliterates it. There are unidentifiable rivers or lakes or reservoirs the color of rust. Everything is the color of ruin. Everything, that is, except for the swimming pools. The pools are small pockets of the perfect color, the color of desire. From above, they appear as crystal beads from a broken necklace, scattered everywhere and sparkling.

Andrea picks me up from the airport, asking absently about the flight. I give her my typical answer: "Takeoff was just awful, but landing was okay." As adults, we are both burdened with identical fears: airplanes, black widows, serial murderers.

In the days since we were growing up here, the Silicon Valley brand name has taken over, displacing any element of actual valley. Silicon Valley seems to eradicate the borders of my childhood, making the valley a nonplace—specifically, not a place of human origin. To me, such development always looks apocalyptic. Half-built buildings spin in my imagination and quickly resemble ruin. Despite having spent twenty-one years here, I find that I am now completely lost if I try to navigate the valley. I will have the slightest memory of how a road gets from one place to another, but then I go blank. My memories are like wet candles—so unable to light that they remain mere urges.

I've been absent from this landscape for ten years, and now I see that Andrea drives like a Californian. She speeds, she's pissed off at people who have not learned the dance of merging, and she rides a person's ass until they move out of her way.

Am I returning home? This is what I've told my friends: "I'm going home for the weekend." But "home" is unrecognizable.

We greet my mom on the curvy apartment complex walkway that leads to a laundry room, a Coke machine, and a gated swimming pool.

My mother is wearing bootleg Levis and a bead necklace around her waist. She looks fantastic; I'm certainly home. That my mother is wearing the latest trendy clothing: this is home to me.

The artifacts of our grand house off Saratoga Avenue are tightly squeezed into her small two-bedroom apartment on Winchester Boulevard. A huge painted photograph of my sister and I when we were little hangs above the old kitchen table. That framed photograph brings with it other rooms—the off-white sunken living room where I was rarely allowed to be and where the portrait hung for years, and the dark brown kitchen I remember as the hub of my youth.

My mother is still trying to block out the California sun. She has installed special blinds to do so, and so, in the middle of summer, all of the lights are on in the apartment. She goads me into talking about Seattle weather and states assuredly that "Seattle is the right climate for me." Something in the way she says "Seattle" proves she is Californian through and through—it doesn't matter if she loves the gray weather, she will always live in this valley.

I turn on the television and start flipping through cable channels. This is acquiescence. On so many previous trips, I have struggled with the setting my sister and mother exist in. I fled this place as I would a minimum-security prison, and it had never made sense to me why they had stayed here.

The truth is, I deserted. Crudely, I left right in the middle of the final call. I moved out of state right at the time they had to put all of our things in boxes, right before I had to meet the new wife, and as my mother was officially impoverished.

I come back now and all things have been sorted. She has recovered well. She sued my father and won. She has retirement money piling up. She has a home, and renting a home seems to have lost its shame. All of her favorite things are around her. Andrea is her family.

WHEN MY MOTHER IS IN THE KITCHEN, the subject drifts to the shore of our father. Andrea was so angry with him when we were young. She saw the injustice and she stuck with it and she sided with my mother. I simply couldn't do that. I had such a difficult and strained time giving up hope for my dad. Recently though, the roles have switched. Andrea is having the correct response at the correct times. She has forgiven; she's unwound the tension of what happened and she talks to my dad, not often, but regularly. My wires are so crossed and misconnected—now that this whole story is over and my mother is completely enjoying her new life, I'm simply unable to call him. He's getting old; I should do it. But months go by, and I don't.

"Dad's pissed at you," Andrea says. "You never call him, he says."

"He never calls me," I respond. "Isn't he supposed to be the dad? Isn't he supposed to be the one to call?"

My mother returns to the room and the topic halts and a new topic is introduced *in medias res*. She tells us there is enough time for the two of us to go to the pool before dinner.

Awkwardly, I suit up in one of my sister's swimsuits. We walk down to the pool and witness a group of teenagers floating on giant rafts. My skin is too pale for the sun anymore. Andrea pokes fun at me.

We agree to dive in simultaneously. The moment when everything turns to water is a sacrament for us both. We both swim to the bottom and rub our hands on the pool's grainy underside. I open my eyes and spend seconds watching Andrea's hair wave above her head. Tiny crystal bubbles frame her eyes. I swim to the deep end, look up at the wobbly California above, and decide to come up for air.

MAC

James Browning

I WAS EATING A CHEESE SANDWICH in the kitchen of our house in Portland, Oregon, when my mother told me she and my father would be getting a divorce. I was in my bunk in my stepfather Mac's boat somewhere off the Maine coast when she told me she and Mac would be getting a divorce, and at a pay phone in a bar in a different part of Portland when my brother told me that she would be getting one from her third husband, Ed. "Was it us?" my brother said. A psychiatrist asked me this after the first divorce—whether I blamed myself—and I said no at once. Our parents were themselves psychiatrists and I believed our mother when she said it was not our fault; our father was depressed and needed time to himself. Now I said, "No, maybe, no," meaning it was *not* us in the case of our father, *may have been* in the case of Mac, was *not* in the case of Ed, who, with seven kids of his own from two previous marriages, sometimes forgot our names.

Mac came to Portland to meet us before marrying our mother but we wouldn't go downstairs. I was eight, my brother was five, and I sent him down when Mac began to climb the stairs. My brother went and came back saying Mac looked like a pirate. I went and my brother had not been exaggerating. Mac wore glasses with a black patch in one of the frames. Blackpatch had been the name of our guinea pig our mother had given away because I let him out like a dog, and, trying to be friendly, I told Mac about Blackpatch. Mac said he hoped I'd learn to take better care of things. Then he asked me if I'd like to move to Connecticut. I thought he had it bad enough with the patch on his eye, so I figured that I should say yes.

It was winter and our flight was the last to take off from the Portland airport before a storm closed it. I'd been crying but this news, delivered by the captain once we were in the air, cheered me up enormously. "Queens," I said when a woman asked where I was going to live. Why lie? I'd never been there, but I thought that only spoiled rich kids lived in Connecticut.

The house was on a hill. My brother got a room downstairs, I got the entire upstairs to myself. Our doors locked from the outside and I wondered if this was Mac's doing. He was a metallurgist and while I'd no idea what that was—my mother said he made springs which got bigger when hot, small again as they cooled—she told a story that made me think Mac could make locks and worse. It was the story of what happened to his eye. A splinter from a piece of wood he'd been sawing had flown up into it. It was a circular saw, which was in the basement and which we weren't allowed to touch. His vision in the bad eye was so distorted that it confused him, which was why he wore the patch.

That first night my mother came upstairs to say goodnight. Then I heard her telling Mac to go up and say it. I felt bad for him—probably he was tired from the drive to pick us up at the airport—and running to meet him I saw him coming up the stairs. His good eye was crusty, red. He asked me if I'd brushed my teeth. I had not but lied because of what he'd said about taking better care of things. "Let's see. Open wide." I opened wide and didn't breathe. He leaned in and smelled my mouth. The hairs in his nose were white. "Why don't you go brush them now?" I went to the bathroom where I ran the water but did not brush my teeth. I came back, said I had, and he said, "That's better."

His company was called Memory Metals because, he said, he'd "taught" the springs to expand and contract the same amount every time. They were used in greenhouses to open and close windows, and in faucets to keep old people and kids from being scalded. I asked if they were in our house.

Mac said, "Man at ten is an animal, at twenty a madman, at thirty a failure, at forty a criminal." (He was fifty-eight, my mother forty-one, and I wondered if the saying really stopped at forty or if he had stopped it there.) He said he'd make a deal with me. He would not treat me like an animal if I did not behave like one. I agreed. A chart appeared with a list of my chores. The dishes I did all right, fires I loved to set and stoke till the flames shot up the chimney, my room I cleaned by kicking everything into the closet as Mac or my mother came upstairs to see if it had been cleaned, dandelions I hid with dirt after he criticized me for not pulling them by the roots. This was the way with us; and finding dandelions where I said I'd weeded, Mac got a pen and added "Laundry" to the chart. But he did it for me when the smell got bad enough.

The chart kept falling down and had to be nailed to the door to the basement. Reading it, I'd hear the whir and the scream of the saw, and I grew up worrying it would get Mac's other eye. Especially if I went to watch and he saw me and looked up. Still I went and what I saw made me think he was insane. Standing over the blade and a box that looked like a birdfeeder, Mac wore his glasses but not safety goggles. How could he not wear them? At the time I thought it was to show the saw who was boss. And I saw a plastic tub filled with what looked like piss. I told my mother about the tub (which she said was beer he had been trying to brew himself) but not about the goggles, as not wearing them seemed like the kind of thing I would do.

The birdfeeder was a big hit with the birds and the squirrels, and then a family of raccoons, after Mac shot all the squirrels with a long brown gun he kept in the library, on a rack between bookshelves. As a joke, I told my brother I was going to shoot Mac. My brother was a tough kid and not one to be trifled with—sitting at the table until it was his bedtime after Mac said he couldn't go until he ate his vegetables— but he just said to let Mac be. I did; for while the gun was frightening, the guts I'd see while mowing the lawn were so frightening that I didn't know what to do. Indeed, the worse things got between Mac and the raccoons, the less inclined I was to act. Mac greased the birdfeeder pole to keep the raccoons from climbing it, but one rubbed dirt on its paws and climbed the pole anyway. Mac put a plastic hemisphere around the pole facing up to keep them from climbing it. Somehow a raccoon got inside the plastic, which was where Mac killed it, and the blood on the sides was like the dregs of wine he'd stir up in his glass.

After he was gone I'd learn that my mother had asked him not to fire the gun while she was with a patient. Otherwise, what did she do about all of this? She said nothing about the gun in front of me, although maybe there was something said late at night when I'd hear them murmuring.

Mac didn't believe in air conditioning and to stay cool in summer I stood under the ceiling fan he'd installed at the head of the stairs. It made my hair stand up, and one time a Memory Metals card in the flat of my hand danced, rose, went through the fan with a violent fluttering, to land in the attic. Going up to get it, I saw a lot of plastic bags. Inside were dirty clothes and records and about nine or ten pornographic magazines. I thought to tell my mother but then opened one and decided to keep them for myself.

The bags belonged to Mac's son Mark, I would learn at the end of that summer when Mark came to live with us. My brother and I had spent the second part of the summer with our father in Oakland, California, in a house with him and our new stepmother Bonnie and her sons Matt and Frank whom we called Fat and Mank. We returned home to find a green tent in the woods at the edge of our property. Mark had lived in the house until my mother said he smelled.

I couldn't tell how old Mark was. He looked about fifteen but had a job with a tree doctor who'd drive up and honk his horn at seven in the morning. Coming home, Mark would grab several bottles of Mac's homemade beer and take them to the tent. Seeing me spying on him from my window, he asked me to bring him beer. I was afraid he knew about me taking his magazines and that he'd yell at me once we were alone. I brought a beer on ice down and saw that Mark had furniture—a wooden desk gone green in parts, a wooden chair in which an *M* was carved. Mark fished the ice out of the glass with two fingers and asked me if I'd like some beer. I thought I'd take to drinking and end up like him if I had more than a sip, and the sip I had tasted like bread which had been a little burnt. I gave it back. I asked Mark what it took to get along with Mac. Mark said he wished he knew. He said Mac's own father had been in the Navy and ran his house as if it were a ship.

A neighbor asked my mother if she smoked marijuana. She did not, and had not seen Mark's marijuana growing in our greenhouse. The next day Mark collapsed the tent, took it and the desk and the chair to work with him, and did not come back. Feeling good about myself—I was not as bad as Mark—I asked Mac what the *M* on Mark's chair stood for. Mac said "Mark."

My question may have been to blame for what happened later that fall—our mother asking Mac to teach us carpentry. My brother went first and spent about ten minutes in the basement with him. I was jealous when I saw the two of them come grinning through the door with an oblong wooden thing. It was a paddle with my name written on the rougher side, my brother's on the smoother one. Mac said it was for hitting us when we were bad. My brother had helped make it and, he'd say, was glad he had because at least he got to choose his side.

HITTING SOMEONE FOR THE FIRST TIME is the hardest, I'd read in a book my mother wrote on child abuse and child sexual abuse. A copy was in our library where I'd see Mac reading it, and where I would read it. A lot of similar books and her files (which I'd never dared to read) were in her office in the front of the house. I'd seen kids I knew going in to see her—one of them was a guy who came to school with bruises on the backs of his legs. Compared to bruises my troubles with Mac did not seem worth mentioning. Certainly it was tempting to go through the office door and tell the doctor about my stepfather, but I thought I could handle him. I was the tallest kid in school and one of the fastest, and I had never asked for help in dealing with older kids.

Mac hit and kicked our dog, Thor, a malamute and supposedly part wolf. And though Thor already hated other dogs, I blamed Mac when he ran away, attacked a neighbor's Doberman, and the neighbors came en masse to say he had to go.

I BURNED THE PADDLE IN THE FIREPLACE, and Mac still had never hit me by the time I went away to boarding school. My best friend had applied, I applied to be with him and—some friend—I went anyway when he did not get in. The school billed itself as the best in the country, and I reminded Mac of this on my way out the door.

It was in Massachusetts. My dorm was a dirty brick building with forty-three other guys, one girl (our house counselor's daughter), a black-and-white TV, a pool table with pockets so torn that the balls fell through and cracked the floor. And while I thought about getting back in the car and going home, I was too proud to say that I'd made a mistake. Watching my mother drive away, I wondered if this was the same reason why she had stayed with Mac.

One of my new neighbors was the second-tallest guy in the building after me. We'd stay up till three or four in the morning asking each other questions from a book of trivia, keeping track of who got the most questions right, simply fighting when we had memorized most of them. Other guys who fought were kicked out after their second offense. We were asked to stop, asked again when we did not; and I would hear later that his family had given a lot of money to the school before and after these warnings. Indeed, the only time I got in trouble that first year was when the school trainer tried to touch my injured knee and I stood up suddenly. He'd been staring at a girl trying to touch her toes; I decided that I didn't want him touching me. He told a dean I'd looked like I wanted to kill him. The dean gave me something called "censure no repeat," meaning I'd be expelled if I behaved this way with faculty or staff again.

I got bad grades and dreaded Mac using this against me. Oddly, he never did, perhaps because my brother picked up where I had left off at home—skipping school to sit in the attic, building fires but then dropping lit matches on the living room carpet to see if it would ignite. Mac convinced my mother to send him to a boarding school for "youth at risk," where he did much better than he had living with us—he got straight As and the title role in their production of *Lil' Abner*.

Alone, Mac and my mother began to rent a boat and go sailing off the coast of Maine. Eventually they bought a boat (people who knew about the patch thought I was kidding when I said the boat was wooden, black) and took my brother and me out. Mac's father had taught him to sail, and I could not see how teaching us to do it would be any different than the time he had taught us carpentry. It was worse. He yelled at us. He yelled at our mother when we went below. Certainly I was big enough to make him stop or to push him overboard, but I thought we needed him to get back to land. We did; and once we were within sight of it, our mother came below and told us that she and Mac would be getting a divorce. Mac stood behind her as if he would tell us, too, leaving no one at the wheel.

MINISKIRT FORAYS

Jill Priluck

IT WAS THE NIGHT OF OUR FIRST SEDER and everyone had finished dipping parsley in the salt water being passed around the table. My sister was sitting to my right at the head of the table. My mother sat across from her on the other end. A few friends were joining us, but tonight my sister's boyfriend, who isn't Jewish, wouldn't be showing up.

The previous night, during the height of the storytelling part of the seder, he had asked why we dwell on suffering. My mother looked my way as if we were speakers on a panel and the moderator had asked a question only I could answer. I said that remembering the bad times makes us more grateful during the good ones. He smiled and shook his head, dissenting. Was it possible that this guy hadn't known suffering? Or was he simply incapable of grasping the concept of learning from suffering? There was a lull.

Tonight was shaping up differently. My mother was hitting it off with my sister's colleague. Extroverted types, they bonded over loving or hating Barbra, Oprah, and the old divas of *Dallas* and *Dynasty*. It was hard to compete with these two gabbers and yet my sister artfully introduced a new topic: her Jewish divorce, also known as a *get*.

"You did *what*?" my mother asked.

"Well *he* didn't care whether we got one or not but *I* did," she said. "If we got married in a Jewish ceremony, why wouldn't we get divorced in a Jewish ceremony?"

She began describing the day she and her ex-husband went for the divorce contract, how they stood in a room with a scribe—he also was a rabbi—and two witnesses. The scribe is obligated to ensure that the parting is willful but he didn't ask anything personal about the breakup. It took about an hour because the scribe wrote the contract using calligraphy. My sister's ex-husband handed the document to her, according to tradition, and they left separately.

Someone at the table interrupted, asking how my sister's ex-husband handled it all.

"It was weird for him but he went along with it. He knew it was what I wanted."

"Daddy and I didn't do that," declared my mother.

No one asked why. I, too, opted to say nothing. After all, my sister was already getting pummeled. Notice my mother's critical tone when my sister describes untangling the post-marital confusion by using a method that didn't involve old clothes and dusty furniture. Why bother intruding? I hadn't been invited to my sister's seder for a Passover rebuke, after all.

Besides, I wasn't surprised by my mother's declaration. Obviously my sister had learned from my parents' mistakes. For my mother and father, divorcing by Jewish law would have been too rational, sure, but also too final. Their inability to accept finality was like a sickness. Yes, they finally signed the requisite civil divorce papers. And yet I don't know where their marriage ends and their lives beyond it begin.

ONE TUESDAY, MY MOTHER HAD picked up my friend and me from school and when we got home the front door of the house was wide open. There had been a burglary, we soon realized. I was half-scared and half-excited.

Couldn't they have taken that ugly, kitschy Buddha-like *tchotchke* upon which my father would place a yarmulke in one of his many efforts to ease tension with humor? My friend and I followed my mother upstairs and nervously surveyed the rummaged-through pantyhose drawer. The crime scene was offering me a worthy diversion.

Beyond the few missing televisions, my mother's wedding ring had been stolen. She had placed it on the windowsill while defrosting hamburger meat in preparation for dinner. Now her calm had degenerated into panic, and she called my father, who arrived just as my friend was being whisked away by *her* worried mother. My dad gave the cops what he could but mostly he just watched everyone. I would spend the afternoon listening to my mom respond to police questioning.

"Was anyone in the house during the day besides you?"

There had been two workers painting the porch.

"But it *couldn't* have been *them*," my mother said.

I was doing my own piecing together. I thought married people never removed their wedding rings. Why did my mother take off hers? And why wasn't the ring in a more secure place when she left the house? Shouldn't she have been more responsible about a ring that had belonged to her mother? And what would replace it? I didn't have the answers and, like the seder two decades later, I didn't ask. I didn't want to upset her even more.

Was that afternoon the prelude to the divorce era? Or had it begun already? Soon after, the adults separated for the first time. I was away at summer camp. By the time I got home they were back together so naturally no one told me about the separation. How many weeks were they apart? What caused it in the first place? I still don't know, even now. I was nine years old then. They wouldn't divorce officially until I was twenty-one. Even then there would be no end to the muddied uncertainty between them.

WHEN I WAS LITTLE I would fantasize about having divorced parents— and glasses, braces, retainers, splints, casts, and other correctives. I wanted a badge that would mark our family defects; a reason for why I was feeling troubled. I wanted to cry with dignity like the *Kramer vs. Kramer* kid whose tantrums were tolerated because his parents were divorcing. But because my parents were married, despite scuffles over getting things done around the house, a few lost tempers, and the occasional flare-up among siblings, from the outside it appeared that as a family we functioned well enough to remain a unit.

There were only one or two kids in my elementary school class with divorced parents. Danielle and her brother Steven lived with their mother Sharon. Sharon's ex-husband Jeffrey lived somewhere else. Danielle was prone to fits of rage and pettiness and I know I wasn't the only one of my classmates who thought that her behavior had something to do with being shuffled from parent to parent. Of course my divorce fantasy didn't accommodate boring technicalities such as custody arrangements.

Another classmate, Michael, lived with his mother somewhere far away from school. His sister Rachel was a year older. Often, she would wear miniskirts. One day, over the intercom, Rachel was called to the principal's office. She would never wear those miniskirts to school again. Secretly, I hypothesized that Rachel had been bending the rules so regularly because she was growing up with a single parent. And while I knew that she didn't belong at the Jewish day school any more or less than I did, for some reason I equated her miniskirt forays with the broken home, even though I myself dared to wear a few. My divorce fantasy was slowly losing its luster.

There was a kid in my brother's class named Ari who used to bully my brother. Ari's mother was a teacher at our school, and she was raising him by herself. No one knew what had happened to Ari's father and no one asked. I'm pretty sure that my parents attributed Ari's awful behavior to his absent father. (Ironically, my brother himself began showing signs of his own difficulties, despite growing up with a very present father.)

Why the lack of compassion? What had become of my need for being marked defective? Had I started seeing Holocaust films at school and concluded that being marked wasn't desirable, necessarily? Probably the emotional balancing act at home was making the prospect of divorce more real even though I doubted that my parents would ever get their divorce act together. Nonetheless I still longed for an identity that would explain why I felt the way I did.

A YEAR OR TWO EARLIER, my mother's father had been hit by a car while taking his evening walk. He died right away. The adults were in Jerusalem on vacation. They got the phone call about the accident in their hotel room and made plans to return immediately.

My mother was beyond grief-stricken. She had depended on my grandpa for advice, sure, but also for the kind of support and affection she never got from her dispirited mother—and now all this had been taken away from her. My mother sought extra compassion and love from my father, who became overwhelmed by her needs. And while she was doing everything she could to cope, the grief would manifest sometimes as anger. There was blame, and the quarrels escalated. My mother never really recovered.

I noticed something else then. The adults would ask my sister her opinion on everything—like whether or not to buy a refrigerator with a built-in ice cube maker, or her thoughts on our overbearing school principal. She was their private expert on practically anything. I didn't get it. Why was her word so valuable? In a way, she was forfeiting her adolescence to compensate for my mother's grief, to put it clinically.

The summer of the quickie separation, my brother had been away, too. Was that the same summer he was kicked out of camp for raiding the girls' area? Maybe. It's hard to nail down the chronology without asking someone. These anecdotes now are just images that have blended together in some unknown sphere of time. But whether it was the separation summer or not, my brother spent the month of August and the following school year glued to the cable box. My parents canceled their subscription because of it, and my brother found other coping strategies such as smoking cigarettes and skipping classes.

I spent as little time at home as I could, preferring the calm order of my best friend's household to the tense topsy-turvy of mine. Outwardly, the adults fought a lot over my dad's jacket and tie combinations, over dinner plans, over my mother's nerves just before we had company.

There's no doubt about it. My mom, a redhead, was a yeller. She would bellow at my father usually until he backed down and apologized for what he'd supposedly done or until he did what she wanted him to do. All those times, he usually was trying to subdue her, to calm her fire. His weapon? Humor. Or even just laughter.

"Oh, sure, make fun. Just keep on making fun," my mother would always say.

Then there would be even more yelling. The adults would criticize each other in front of us. My mother would do it outright with insults, and my father with jokes. Then she would get angry and start yelling and my father would leave the room. I never learned from them how to resolve arguments.

It was so rare for my father to raise his voice that the few times he did yell were scary. In those instances, his only reprieve was leaving; usually he'd sleep at 1355, a relative's apartment building. He'd always be back the next evening after work, showered and shaved and smelling of Chaps.

One Rosh Hashanah, I was sitting in the living room filling candy dishes. All I heard were the words "I want a divorce." They were fighting over nothing and when I say that, I mean they were fighting over practically nothing, like perhaps my father lowering the heat on the simmering sweet-and-sour stuffed cabbage.

The adults were evolving into polar opposites. On the Sabbath, my father would rest at home and my mother would play tennis in the morning and perhaps take us somewhere in the afternoon. (She will go out for ice cream or cheesecake at midnight on a moment's notice.) My dad would rise early and say the morning prayers while my mother would sleep late when time allowed. Drinking the day's first cup of coffee was her form of worship. My father saved while my mother spent—though neither could ever turn down a good bargain. He would eat strictly kosher food, always. She would eat anything whenever. Lobster. Shrimp. Spare ribs. Always outside the home, natch. To the adults, these differences probably seemed like harmless navigable tics when they got married. To my sister, my brother, and me, they stood out like rusty beer cans in a woodsy ravine.

Sometime in the early 1980s, about a decade before my parents finally would reach Splitsville, I remember feeling that percussionist Bruno in the movie (and subsequent television series) *Fame* had a more stable family life than mine, despite his being raised just by his dad. The love between Bruno and his dad practically oozed off the screen and I longed for this unerring simplicity.

More than a million kids at that time were watching their parents' divorces unfold. News reports sensationalized the trend and soon divorce itself was under assault. In 1989, Judith Wallerstein would publish the landmark twenty-five-year *Second Chances* study, claiming that divorce was wreaking havoc on kids, and so-called profamily groups would make Wallerstein's study their rallying cry. As these debates swirled, my parents' stance was simple. They thought divorce was detrimental to young children. However, in this position they neglected a related hypothesis, that living with parents who fought a lot wasn't one of the building blocks for positive child development either.

BY THE TIME I REACHED HIGH SCHOOL, the adults had become more of a nuisance than ever. Eating together was rare. Neither my sister nor my brother was living at home. I fended for myself. Usually, my dad went to an evening aerobics class (he was the only guy in the class then), return tiredly refreshed and perhaps fall asleep while watching television. My mother watched the local and network news, then *Wheel of Fortune*, *Jeopardy*, and maybe *Entertainment Tonight*. Sometimes I ate with her. Sometimes I ate at a friend's house. But if I ate with the adults, it wasn't simple.

"Where should we go?" my mother would say.

"I don't know—wherever you want to go," my father would respond.

"Why don't you suggest something? I always decide where we're going."

He would name a place.

"I don't want to go there. We always go there."

"Then let's go somewhere else."

"I don't want to go anymore. Let's just stay home."

Eventually my mother's hunger would bristle and they would settle on someplace. It's hard to say how much they didn't like spending time together. A lot of married people don't like each other after a while, right? Certainly, the adults *loved* each other very much. But they didn't seem to *like* each other. And they'd spend these dinners talking about other people's problems.

"Oh, there's Eleanor Blaustein. She's not with Larry. They separated six months ago, you know."

My dad would nod.

"Oh, I wonder who she's dating," my mother would continue, peeking across the room to get a half-glimpse of the mysterious dinner date.

I wouldn't say anything. I figured that fixating on someone else's crumbling relationship was easier than conquering their own disintegrating marriage. Instead my mind would wander. Whatever happened to comparisons between marriage and roller coasters? Why didn't either of my parents declare how much they loved each other, despite the rough patches? What ever happened to dealing bravely with one's problems? And why did my parents seem so passive about their need for love and emotional fulfillment?

I had always wanted to protect my parents from feeling unhappy or guilty about their turmoil. I never got arrested or trashed a car. The lowest grade I got was a C in history my freshman year and that was because I felt intimidated by the teacher, a very tall, overly bright gay man with blond hair and a Ph.D. I don't even know if the adults realized I was depressed. In fact they probably blamed my moods on adolescent angst. Besides, they were too preoccupied with their own problems to realize what was going on around them.

Maybe I'm making things sound worse than they were. Being together as a family wasn't always stressful. We went on trips to bird sanctuaries, the circus, and petting zoos; we went downtown to see the tall ships and up north to the mountains. My parents were all family all the time. Other parts of their lives were secondary to their primary roles as parents. And that's why they didn't do anything about ending their marriage predicament. But this is also the reason things were so confusing.

Sometime that year when my mother was away again with her friend Paula (Paula would divorce later, too), my brother, my sister, Dad, and I congregated at my brother's apartment.

"I know. We can't seem to get along," my father said.

"So get separated," said my sister nonchalantly. "We can handle it."

My dad looked at me, his brown eyes sad with regret.

"Yep," said my brother. "Look, if you don't get along . . ."

"But would you guys be okay with that?" my dad said, again looking at me.

I was the one who, after the adults, would be most impacted by the decision. My sister, then happily married, was living in another city. My brother was in college and had already set up a life apart from my parents. But I was still living with them. And yet I followed the consensus of my brother and sister. Where was my ego when I needed it most?

"What else can you do?" I said. "You guys are always fighting. You don't like being together."

It seemed like my dad was going to cry. He kept looking at me, seeking perhaps some kind of white-towel surrender that would end this talk of divorce. But I looked away and pretended that I didn't care, that the matter was settled.

Was I angry that deciding our family's future suddenly seemed to lie in my lap when it should have lay more immediately in the laps of my parents? Was I thinking, don't parents usually make the decision and then tell the kids instead of making the decision *with* the kids? Was I secretly distressed that my mother wasn't present for this would-be family summit? Did I feel bad that I couldn't express my real feelings, opting instead for a veneer of strength? Was I bothered that my dad was consulting us when he should have been talking to my mother?

Yes.

Over the next summer, it was their twenty-fifth anniversary. I was in California with two friends. In a few days, we would be driving to Sequoia National Park. I didn't tell my friends about the big anniversary or that my mother was away with Paula while my father was at home working during the day and spending his nights watching television on the porch. I agonized over whether or not to call the adults. Instead I called my mother on her forty-sixth birthday two days later.

The months passed and I left for college. Three weeks later, while I was on the phone with my mother, I asked her to get Dad for me. She said he wasn't home. When I asked where he was she said she didn't know. When I asked whether he was at aerobics she said that he wasn't living with her anymore, that he hadn't been there for several weeks and that he was staying at 1355.

My mother wouldn't ever *say* they were separated but if that's what they were, then in a way I was relieved. Obviously my presence at home had been keeping them from parting. Why couldn't my mother be more straightforward? And why hadn't my dad called to tell me what was happening? Being a thousand miles away I was already feeling destabilized, and since things at home had been so drawn out for so long, in a way it didn't feel like anything had changed. I mean, it's not like I wanted an invitation to their separation party, but I did need an acknowledgment from them that I wasn't getting. I got a sense that it really was the end of their marriage, but I didn't know for sure if this was another short-term split or the real thing.

By Thanksgiving, my mother the newly separated empty nester had met some tennis player named Herb. At least she wasn't dating this Herb before the separation, some would say. But there had been other platonic Herbs who used to keep my mother company—like her friend Chico who would take her for lunch or to a museum and my dad never seemed to care.

For months my father would only call me from work during the day. When I asked him where he had moved, he wouldn't say. If I needed to talk to him at night, I couldn't reach him. One day I broke down and demanded to know where the hell he was living. He finally disclosed that he had moved in with a woman he met at aerobics. I think he was ashamed.

Perhaps I should be grateful that the rift between my parents wasn't messier. Neither of them ever left. They never abused us or each other. They wouldn't become entangled in a court fight and they would never date or remarry serially. But is it so bad to wish they had handled things differently? After all, there are parents who deal with their kids honestly. Parents who take care of their kids' emotional needs before their own. Parents who confront their problems and actually *solve* them. No, my situation wasn't all that bad. I had two parents who loved and supported me. We lived well. But despite the custom-made couches and glass chandeliers, we internalized the sense of pressure and defeat that often permeated the household.

The following school year ended with my grandmother's death. Her funeral was one of the first times I saw my parents together since they parted. In the foyer of the funeral home, my mother's new boyfriend awkwardly greeted my father who slipped away uncomfortably. It was sad in the chapel, sitting alongside my mother, sister, and brother. My dad was standing in the back of the room.

The new boyfriend had emerged earlier that year and already he was living with my mother—and me, now that I was home for the summer. One night while I was sleeping a glass lamp fell on me. In the morning I showed my mother the cut on my face. She insisted on taking me to the emergency room, after consulting the new boyfriend. I hadn't wanted to go anyway but now that *he* was involved, I was aggravated even more. He wasn't my dad and he barely even knew me—or my mother at that point. But we went, and soon after arriving, my mother had a fight with the attending physician. She insisted on seeing a plastic surgeon. He was young and kind of cute and as I lay there on the gurney with a split above my lip I was glad he was there with me. Maybe the scar on my face from that day was the kind of mark I had been seeking as a child. Over and over that summer, death would preoccupy my thoughts as if I were in mourning. I guess the adults had ceased living as I had always known them: together.

I felt that I couldn't get too close to people for fear of ruining them, needing too much, or simply exploding with anger. I would long for a life somewhere else, in Nepal, Thailand, California, anywhere that was far away from everyone. I couldn't involve friends in this despair really and even though I wanted to separate myself from all the changes that were happening, it held sway in everything I did. I was accused of being selfish, difficult, or just plain bitchy. For a long time, I would seek out men I could keep at arm's length.

I couldn't remember a time when I had been content. I still can't. And compared to my divorce-free peers, I have needed more time and space to grow. I had more work to do: I had to overcome the past and create a path for myself. For the most part, my friends with divorced parents had contended with their situations. But I couldn't get over it because for years and years there seemed to be no real end, no closure. And there still wasn't.

My mother moved all of my personal belongings while I was abroad the following year. Not only was she selling the house but she was also moving to Florida with the guy. At the same time, a strange arrangement between my mother and father was developing. My father asked my mother to send all of the stuff she didn't want to 1355, which supposedly belonged to my father, who was staying a half-mile away. She would be staying in the apartment during visits. Suddenly it seemed as if they were building a new home together, with all the household stuff that my mother hadn't taken to Florida. This time, however, neither of them would be living there. They were incubating two lives, one in which they'd acknowledge the split, another in which their lives together would continue.

I would first see the flat upon returning from overseas. It was filled with furniture, kitchen supplies, and *tchotchkes* from the house. My

belongings were packed in brown boxes, strewn about one of the rooms. My dad looked sad as he watched me surveying the damage. I obsessed that my mother had read my private writings. And that day I chastised my father for everything that had happened. I told him how much the two of them sucked and how lonely I felt. And in a way I felt that he was crying with me.

My mother in those days never seemed to get enough love from my sister, my brother, and me. I would feel guilty and undeserving when I didn't indulge her aggravating claims of never seeing us or of not knowing us anymore. She would act as though her family had abandoned her, when really her marriage had ended—supposedly. My mother relies on me to console her, still, as if we were close friends, not mother and daughter. And even though I never would feel free to break away completely from the adults, I desperately needed to let them go somehow.

I went back to school for a class, and spent the rest of the summer cloaked in a sadness I didn't quite understand. I read *The Autobiography of Malcolm X* and *Native Son* and I'd be reassured that one could find pain in almost every aspect of life, not just in the breakup of a family.

Every time I go home now I stay in this same apartment where I first saw my belongings in boxes. The apartment hasn't changed much even though it's been almost eight years. It's spotted with the same furniture, pictures, dishes, and books from my youth. A large oil painting by a family friend (my mother has its twin in Florida and always hated the painting my father liked so much). A ten-inch RCA television that my mother would watch while cooking. Six or seven of my mother's coats. (She wears them during her visits.) A two-by-two mosaic she bought in Italy, featuring Snoopy, in a "Lechaim!" or "To life!" toast with Woodstock (Woodstock's bubble features several question marks). The cummerbund my father wore to my brother's bar mitzvah. The bow tie he wore to my bat mitzvah. My parents' first bedroom set, a brown-paneled wood of a not-so-special variety. Half of the adults' wedding album. My mother has the other half, I believe. Her wedding-day portrait leans against the wall in a dusty corner.

Most of it is fodder for an attic. My mother badgers my father to throw out everything (except for her wedding-day portrait) but my father won't comply. To him, they are remnants worth keeping. So the formerly married pair will fight over the telephone and the stuff sits. Then my mother comes for a visit and the two spend an afternoon together discarding things in trash bags, bickering, laughing and reliving long-past moments, like the time she wore the fur-trimmed gold and brown miniskirt dress on one of their first dates in the 1960s.

Funny how they now bond over clothing when before, it instigated arguments. Funny how my mother stores her things in the apartment. Funny how the adults still haven't been to any event, graduation, or holiday table together (save for my grandmother's funeral) side-by-side with their new partners.

Kids of divorce are supposedly less emotionally resilient than their divorce-free counterparts. They have different stories from each other, but often suffer similarly from conditions gleaned from the pages of pop psychology treatises such as *The Dance of Anger*. Fear of intimacy. Inability to solidify relationships. Quick to cut off from loved ones. I still don't completely know how being the child of an up-and-down-marriage-and-eventual-divorce has affected me but, yes, I've seen some of these character traits firsthand. In my circle of friends, just as many kids of divorced parents as kids of intact marriages are getting married. Obviously none of us know which marriages will last.

Is a forever-lasting marriage necessarily the goal? Jewish law prescribes that each man and woman has a soul mate, usually the person she or he chooses to marry. If a married couple never finds peace, tradition holds that they should separate. Otherwise problems accumulate and, ultimately, consume the pair. To be sure, Jewish law doesn't take divorce lightly. But the freedom to divorce creates a stronger marriage bond by making it one of will and consent, not obligation or compulsion. And once divorced, each half is free to find their real soul mates.

Of course, in the Talmud it says that when there's a divorce, the heavens are crying.

There's a period in every divorce of posturing, of being childish, of not respecting all the kids involved. There are untruths. Missteps. Generally irresponsible behavior. There's evading. Avoiding. Mishandling. Maybe these determine the extent to which the divorce lingers and creates lifelong patterns. Maybe the answer lies in the tangible twists and turns.

My parents had always felt ashamed of divorcing. Their guilt was like a shawl they could never remove. Do all couples go through a period, however silently, of fearing finality? Or is this often simply a blink-of-an-eye moment compared with the more important need for space and ultimately closure? Probably my parents were paralyzed by fear. Maybe they knew a divorce wouldn't resolve their feelings about each other. Maybe they thought we wouldn't be able to handle it. Maybe they didn't think they could handle it.

Just days before this year's seders, I met my mother at her hotel the afternoon she arrived for her spring visit. We ate lunch then headed back to her room only to find my father in the lobby, suitcase in hand. My thirtieth birthday had been a few days earlier and my parents planned a surprise visit so we could celebrate together. That night we went to dinner (my brother was the only one missing) and said goodbye just before midnight. My parents would spend the whole night in the same hotel room talking and would have breakfast together in the morning before my father returned home for the Passover holiday.

In some ways the adults will always be more intertwined than not. They still argue. Just not about the everyday. But it's still a bizarre, unrelenting romance of a sort that will never die. Jewish law says they are still married. And that's fine with me.

FLOATING BRIDGE

Matt Briggs

WHEN I WAS YOUNGER, my father used to rock me for hours in his rocking chair. Once, while drinking his second forty ounces of malt liquor he puked on me, and I jumped down from the chair and ran into the kitchen. "Mom, Dad spilled on me." I don't remember the actual incident, but I recall my mother telling the story as a cute family anecdote. Later, it became a harsh addition to her portrayal of my father as a drunk, a drug addict, a man damaged by a hard childhood. It became just another example of why she left him.

A story she tells less often is about how I barely survived a car accident at the base of the hill we lived on. My parents briefly had a Volkswagen bug. As they drove down the hill, another car racing across the hill plowed into our car. My mother, who held me on her lap, smashed the windshield with the crown of her head. Somehow the force of the crash threw me clear of the wreck and into a maple on the corner. I don't know who was at fault in the collision. I don't even remember jarring loose from my mother's lap and floating through the air and passing through branches until I stuck like a stray kite. I do remember my mother sometimes pointing to the maple. "There's the tree that saved your life," she'd say.

We lived in a starter house on Southwestern above Lincoln Park in West Seattle. The house sat on the side of the hill looking over the

Duwamish Valley and toward the hazy, white caps of the Cascade Mountains. My mother painted the kitchen with brilliant orange and yellow latex. On my bedroom wallpaper, animals caroused in a psychedelic jungle. We moved out of the place in the early seventies, against my mother's wishes, to a rundown Fall City farmhouse that my father had found in a cedar thicket fifty miles from Seattle. We kept the place in West Seattle as a rental. My father was too nostalgic and too thrifty ever to sell anything with memories and future equity. Much of the house rotted during the damp Pacific Northwest winters when my father's first tenant handed it over to his dealer as a flophouse. My mother called it a flophouse, now it would be called a crack house. Same thing. Junkies rather than drunks stored themselves there while they got stoned and used the toilet when they weren't constipated. There were similarities between all of my father's houses and a crack house. A house my father lived in and a crack house were both places to essentially contain bodies and keep them out of the rain; both were cold storage for stoned bodies rather than homes and places to live.

I don't remember the city house as any place except as the place I lived when I was a baby. I have photographs of myself in the house and photographs of my mother and father, both much skinnier and younger than I am now. I have a series of photographs of my father making saucy eyes, his emaciated and pallid chest brushing up against the orange walls. In one picture, he wears a white terry-cloth bathrobe and has a bushy mustache and bushy Beatlesque hair and leans forward and pouts at the camera. My mother, too, is young and silly and smiles comfortably— rather in contrast to her current faint, stressed mock smile. In one photograph, my mother wears a thick fake fur coat she says she found at St. Vincent de Paul. She has wire rim glasses and a toothy smile and displays a sleek, nylon-clad leg. In these photographs, my parents are young and at times stylish and urban, and, well, happy.

Maybe happiness depends on wholeness. All I can see in these photographs now is evidence of the impending fracture. The roots of what would make my parents unhappy were there already. However at twenty-four and twenty, things like his hangovers and his limited nature and her erratic depression and her constant dissatisfaction seemed like small things, irrelevant things, actually, compared to a tidy little house on a hill overlooking Puget Sound and the Cascade and Olympic mountain ranges, a newborn, and a good enough job as a waitress or short-order cook. This was just the beginning. Life was bound to get better from then on. On the ground floor, life promised to be a vast mansion they could get lost in.

I guess they got lost.

THE SUCCESSION OF HOUSES alternated between my mother's houses and my father's houses. Looking back now, it seems we lived in a dizzying succession of houses. At each place, though, it seemed that we had finally settled, that this was it, this would be our last move and our lives could finally progress. After the West Seattle house, we lived through most of the seventies in a country house in a little town just below the Snoqualmie Falls. This house, hidden at the end of a macadam road in a clump of cedar trees, was my father's house. It was a place people had trouble finding by the address. It required the driving directions, go down the Fall City Preston road until you come to the pink steel girder bridge (someone had painted it with Army surplus paint) and then take the next right and drive to the end of the road. Our house is just below the pasture with the white ten by one fence. We moved from this house in 1981 to a suburban house near the interstate. This was my mother's house, a large, just constructed two-story with outdoor lamps, a two-car garage, a dining room, a rec room, the smell of new paint and carpet. My father prevailed after we had lived in the house for only two years and moved us to another farmhouse set back from the road out on the North Fork of the Snoqualmie. When Mom left this house, she didn't take my father or us with her.

After we moved to the country, my father sometimes took me to Seattle on his motorcycle in the mornings while the streets were still damp. I had a white helmet with a leather buckle and the snaps were so tight, when I pressed them together my fingers ached and then the chrome tips bit together. Mom had bought the helmet in a thrift store in Renton, a white one for me and a green one with metal specks for my brother. I wore a sweater and a jean jacket. His motorcycle wasn't like the colossal chrome and machines his biker friends drove—hogs or horses, his friends called them. Dad never mentioned to them that he had a motor bike as well. He kept his Honda hidden under a blue tarp. The Honda made a steady hum like a newly tuned lawn mower. In the fresh morning rain, I sat behind Dad clutching his waist, my nose buried in his leather jacket, shedding specks of leather. I had to be careful of the long muffler because it raised blisters if I brushed my calf against the blue hot chrome. I put my boot sole on it. I kept my eye on it. We raced down the hill and the bike made a whirring noise and then, as it picked up speed, the whirring dropped down and we raced over the freeway, our feet inches from the flickering cement. On the floating bridge, moss grew over the concrete. In the puddles that collected on the worn shoulders, I could see the tiny agates and feldspar in the old cement. The lake smelled of open water and seagulls and fish and diesel fuel and then we passed through a tunnel with totem poles pressed into the cement and the words *Portal to the Pacific*, and that meant we were in Seattle.

The excitement of racing to Seattle clutching my father's leather jacket dropped off when we went up a row of bungalows and stopped, not at the freshly painted houses with the swing set visible in the backyard, but at the house with the dog crap–studded yellow lawn. A bleary-eyed guy met us at the door and we all sat down in the living room. Dad sold him lid and smoked a joint with him while I waited on the couch. Afterwards, it was easy to talk Dad into stopping at a hamburger place and getting fries and a milkshake and we ate them from the bags. Sometimes, we bought fried chicken and Rainier cherries from the International District and then drove down to the waterfront and ate them in the grass between the Alaskan Viaduct (a hissing double-decker cement eyesore and rebuttal to the Kool-Aid blue Sound and the hazy, snow-capped peaks of the Olympics) and the waterfront that then still had wharves with ships unloading crates as well as the long warehouses being converted into restaurants and retail stores.

IN THE MID-1970S, my father sold dope mostly to his friends, people he'd known for years. Usually they arrived on Saturday before my father went to work in Seattle where he was the Copper Kitchen's night cook. His friends knocked on the door and always seemed to have spontaneously come out to the country. They sat down and Dad asked them if they'd like a joint. "Sure. What a good idea," his friends said. They passed the joint around and their talk slowly drifted away. They grunted and wheezed and my dad put something on the record player. "I know this. I know this. It's what's-his-name."

"Yeah," Dad said. And finally after the smoke started to drift out the windows they said, "This is good shit. Do you know where I can get some? It's dry in Seattle. Dry as a bone." And this made everyone laugh and cough at the same time. And Dad grabbed a baggie from the crumpled brown paper bag he kept in a kitchen drawer next to the potatoes. They handed him a folded bill and he handed them a lid and then a few minutes later they stood and stretched and said, "It's been a blast."

Dope then had a benignly illicit quality, similar to jaywalking or California stops at stop signs. Everyone my parents knew had a stash and everyone, it seemed, referred to the police as pigs. People smoked dope in parks and at concerts without huddling furtively around their pipes. They brought out thick, heavy joints and tossed the roaches into the ditch. Weed, everyone knew, wasn't addictive. It wasn't even a real drug.

But by the late 1970s, the pigs had begun to crack down. They changed the sentencing laws. They officially designated marijuana a gateway drug, a door to the criminal underworld. But the hip had already moved through the gateway to the real stuff, and the unhip had moved on to houses and careers and PTA meetings. My father found himself selling the weed he didn't manage to smoke himself to a dwindling roster of friends and finally to a high school–aged dealer who drove a blue-glitter '57 Chevy.

My mother asked Dad to stop selling. "It's not worth it," she said. "For your own use is fine. But they're taking people's houses now. If you keep dealing, I'll leave you."

She didn't get out before they busted him. In 1978, my father sold a grocery bag of dope to an FBI officer and ended up in jail. He spent three months on a work-release program and then had to see a probation officer once a month for three years. My father spoke of his probation officer with not a little pride. "I've got to go see my PO," he said. He had places to go, people he had to see.

Mom felt his conviction was a good thing. She thought they could discard my father's rural dope-dealing fantasy and begin to live their real lives. Mom went to Bellevue Community College and when she graduated, she found a job at Boeing, earning twice my father's pay. Within six months, my father found a new job as a county bus operator earning slightly more than Mom. At my mother's instigation, they bought a new house in a subdivision on the South Fork of the Snoqualmie River.

The new house had a garage built on a cement slab. The new house had two stories and a dining room with a chandelier that required special light bulbs shaped like candles from the True Value hardware. It had three bedrooms, a laundry room, and a connection to the city sewer. My father stood in the driveway and muttered that the neighbors were close enough to hear him take a crap.

As soon as we moved, my father rented the Fall City house to one of his long-standing customers, Mike McCree. Mike sold fake and real marijuana at concerts and had been an intermittent heroin junkie and cokehead. Except for the selling of catnip and rosemary, he had everything else in order—a steady job as a cook and a twenty-two-year-old girlfriend. To mark the occasion of the rental, we went out to dinner with Mike and his girlfriend, Trudy, to a Mexican restaurant in Bellevue. My parents knew Trudy from before Mike. She'd been a young waitress at the Copper Kitchen.

We waited on the red tile and listened to the business men eat their late suppers. We (the landlords) were going to sit down and have a nice business-like dinner with our new tenants. My mother had already noted that we could deduct it as a business expense.

Trudy was on cocaine. This has the feeling of an accusation now. She was coked to the gills. I was eleven years old and already nervous to be with my parents in this den of 1980s new and affluent Bellevue. Trudy laughed with the sound of a manic jug band singing saw player, the noise splitting out of her rack of crooked teeth. The sound vibrated and warbled through the room. She wore long black leather boots with thick square heels and a skirt that left a band of skin exposed at her calves and a white blouse with a black tie around it. Her hair was long, but her face came out of the hair with its long broken nose, stark black eyebrows, black eyes, and swollen lipsticked lips. Mike McCree had hooded eyes and leaned forward to eat his refried beans and smiled to himself as we talked. Trudy told long stories I couldn't follow. At eleven, I could only follow the sound of her laugh cutting through the room and people looking over at our table. It seemed almost as if they stood up and circled our table and stared, but really I suspect they just glanced in our general direction and perhaps wondered after Trudy laughed if a sewer cap had blown free and was rolling down the street.

On the way home, my mother was pissed. She didn't want to rent to them. She thought they were disgusting and grotesque and lowlifes. She was glad she and my dad had put their lives in order.

"At least they are real people," my father said.

WHEN MY FATHER'S PROBATION ENDED in 1983, he bought two halide lights, a bucket of white paint, and a pallet of plywood. He converted the garage into a growing room and understood now, after meeting knowledgeable marijuana cultivators in jail, how to start from quality seeds and how to trick the female plants into bearing sticky, heavy buds.

The air in the garage filled with steam and spores. The industrial lights gave off a heavy, constant bass hum. Unlike the ragweed he'd been growing before, which he'd been able to smoke every couple of hours, when he sampled his new crop, his face went slack and he stared into space for a while and finally, lazily, stood up. After harvest, he sold his entire crop to a distributor. Whereas before he'd had a kind of hobby of growing dope, he now had a small business.

It didn't take long for him to want to move again to more remote digs. The neighbors around here are nosy, he said. They don't mind their own business. The neighbors are always watching us. We rented out the new house and bought another old farmhouse, leaving behind my brother's and my own bedrooms, leaving behind wall-to-wall carpets, abandoning any sense that things would ever get better. The new house was tiny, with an attic that had been converted into two small bedrooms. An adult couldn't stand up there, but my brother and I could stand in the center of the rooms. The main amenity was that it had a gigantic windowless basement. My father bought two more halide lights and filled the basement with a dense jungle of bloated THC-bearing plants. My mother reminded my father of her promise to leave him if he continued to sell. He just shrugged. This was who he was. The underlying tension between my mother and father had been present from the moment my father moved her out to the country. It had been something my brother and I had grown up with.

For work, Mom wore a turquoise suit, black nylons, and high-heel shoes that came down to dime-size points. She wore her Boeing badge, displaying her wide, toothy smile. She left the house in a flurry at five-thirty in the morning and when I woke to get ready for school, I could still smell her perfume hanging in the air. Her shoes left divots in the hardwood floor as if someone had taken a ball peen hammer and played war drums from the bedroom to the kitchen, from the kitchen to the front door.

My father drove the bus at night and woke during the day while I was at school and then didn't come home until I had gone to bed. He had low seniority and so rarely had weekends off. On his days off, he wore a jean jacket with the fleece lining coming out at the collar and cuffs, a plaid work shirt with his Zigzags and Zippo lighter in his breast pocket, and rawhide work boots from the bus company store. He wore his long hair wrapped in rubber bands. His ponytail hung down his back.

My brother and I rarely saw our parents together, then. In hindsight it might seem as if they had already separated.

One day Dad noticed the dime-size holes my mother's heels had left in the floor. He called my brother and me downstairs to explain ourselves.

"I didn't do it," my brother said.

"I didn't do it," I said.

And then he looked at the marks. "That fat bitch," he said.

During spring break, my father took his vacation and instead of spending time with my mother, he took my brother and me up the Elwah in the Olympic Mountains. We camped the first night at the Anderson Farm, which had posters outside that said, "Do not sleep within a hundred yards of this historic shelter." We slept inside it on the hardwood floor. In the morning, Dad heated coffee on his propane stove and we hiked for miles through the forest and finally turned around on a bridge over some tributary to the Elwah, miles up the trail at the base of a mossy cleft.

We came home the Sunday before school started again. There was no sign of my mother except for the divots in the hardwood floor. She had moved out.

On Monday, I awoke, showered, and put on my clothes. My brother stayed in bed.

"Aren't you going to school?"

"No."

I waited at the bus stop alone and when the bus came, I took a seat near the back and looked out at the swamp near the house and then the bus went down the road and over the Middle Fork Bridge and then the North Fork Bridge and then finally over the Snoqualmie River Bridge where we pulled into the elementary schoolyard. I just kept staring out the window at my faint reflection in the glass. I glanced at the other kids to see if they knew. They were talking, and when the bus stopped, everyone stood up and shuffled out of the bus. I didn't get up until they were almost all out, and then I went inside the classroom. I could hear them outside playing soccer in the damp field. Mr. Johnson sat at his desk drinking coffee. He didn't look up. "It's still recess," he said.

I sat at my desk and took out my homework.

It had finally happened. That was all I could think. It had finally happened, this thing that happened to other kids had happened to me. An enormous gap had opened up. My life had seemed complicated enough—all the complications of my reading group, of my friends, of the kids I didn't get along with, the constant struggle just to get through the sixth grade, a grade I had been looking forward to since kindergarten when in general assembly the sixth graders stood against the wall at the back of the gym. The boys even had slight mustaches. They all wore blue jeans and jackets and whispered through the entire assembly. They could do pretty much what they wanted except not come to school. Sixth grade, for me, hadn't been simple like that. It had involved at first moving into the old farmhouse and then . . . this.

Coming home after school had meant returning to an empty place. My brother usually came home on a separate bus. When I got home, I would usually cut myself some Tillamook cheddar and watch the *League of Justice*. But when I came home that day, my brother and Dad sat in the kitchen. Mud and moss covered their jeans. They had been hiking. My father asked me why I'd gone to school. I'd been looking forward to falling into my old, reassuring routine and now that was gone just like everything else.

"Today is a school day," I said.

"Don't you know what's happened?"

I shrugged. I knew what had happened. Mom had left. She was gone when we came home from the Olympic Mountains. She left as if she had just been visiting. She had been saying she was going to leave and now she had done it. It was clear what had happened. I just couldn't really understand all of it. For instance, why did her leaving mean not going to school?

"She left me for some guy she met at her job," Dad said. "Some pencil prick."

I went upstairs and played video games.

After a while, my brother came upstairs and lay on his bed with his hands folded on his chest and stared up at the sky out of his bedroom window. I stopped playing my game and then lay on my bed and looked up at the clouds, too.

"Are you going to school tomorrow?" my brother asked.

"I'm not sick," I said.

"I'm staying home with Dad. He needs me."

MY FATHER TRANSFORMED INTO A SNIFFLING and humble man. He didn't smoke or drink anything for the two weeks Mom was gone. He listened to my brother and me. I thought maybe this had really scared him. Maybe he had really stopped smoking and then maybe Mom and he would get back together. On the phone, it sounded like Mom was just about to come back. She talked to us and told us how much she missed us. She talked to Dad and he said to her, "I love you, too." And then finally he said, "Well, you know I'll say I'll quit but when it comes down to it, once I get the girl back, I'll have the girl and the dope. You know, that's just how I am." They talked for a little longer, but Mom never did show up.

At last, they met at Denny's to talk about what was going to happen next. Mom sat under a wall of brass sculpture. She had a Tab. Dad sat down and we sat down and they began to talk. It seemed like maybe somehow they had worked things out.

"I've been so upset," Dad said. "I haven't been able to smoke or drink in two weeks."

"You really have stopped," Mom said. "I can tell."

"Isn't that what you wanted?"

Mom told Dad that my brother and I would go to live with her after the school year. My father shook his head. "You're going to take them away from their home?"

"I don't want to go," my brother said.

"I don't think you can take them away from their home," Dad said. "To live with you and your boyfriend."

"Do you really want to get legal about this? A convicted drug dealer who has a basement full of pot is telling me he can keep my kids."

"Are you threatening me?"

"I'm just telling you, you don't have a leg to stand on."

"It's not like you didn't profit from it too. You are just as guilty as I am."

"You promised me you wouldn't grow it again after your probation. Look, Ron," Mom said, "I'm not going to do anything. You can do whatever you want. The children can visit you. But they aren't going to live in that house anymore."

"You left me to sleep with that guy and then you try to cast me as the bad guy?" His emptied an ice cube from his water glass, rolled in his mouth and then crushed it.

DAD HAD STOPPED GOING TO WORK. We went to the King County Pool in Issaquah to swim every other night. On the drive there, Dad listened to a tape of *Sergeant Pepper's Lonely Hearts Club Band* and shook his head. "This used to sound good," he said. "This used to really be something when I first heard it." And he kept listening to the album on the long drive from the house to the pool. We left at dusk. Fog lay out on the road from the rivers and floated in from the dairy fields. When we parked at the pool, it seemed like everyone had gone elsewhere and we were now alone in the world.

Once we went inside, I could smell the thick chlorine and hear shouts that echoed up against the tiled walls. We changed in the locker room and pinned the bright orange keys attached to safety pins to our shorts. The pebble floor felt rough and knobby on the soles of my feet. My father swam laps while my brother and I horsed around in the shallows and then when we got bored with that, we would climb up onto the diving board and do cannonballs into the deep end, stinging our backs. The neighborhood kids did flips or smooth eel-like drops into the water. We performed loud, ominous plunges into the water; the bubbles swirled around us forcing water into our noses.

MOM MOVED TO RENTON, a suburb rolled into the endless tracks of once forested land south of Seattle. The boxy house sat across from a water tower in a subdivision linked with sidewalks and large green power transformers and empty playgrounds with creosote log jungle gyms and wood chips. Someone had sprayed "Renton Pigs Suck" on the water tower, and the stoners in the middle school where I started that fall sometimes called my neighborhood *Renton Pigs Suck*.

Mom lived with Mike Thomas, who my brother and I knew from her parties as that geeky guy who drank too much. He was a thin, blonde Irish man. He wore striped dress shirts with a mechanical pencil sticking out of the pocket. Once we had gone to Snoqualmie Falls with him and his then-wife. On the way back, she told us about Ireland. "It looks just like this place except there are no trees," she said.

The basement of this new house was unfurnished and the upper story had three bedrooms and two baths and a rickety porch. Behind the house, Mike Thomas had a vegetable garden where he grew lettuce and leeks and Brussels sprouts. Overgrown patches of peppermint, sage, and rosemary smelled faintly like pizza in the backyard. His yard had been mowed to a scruffy flat turf. He'd planted grass seeds in the hard pan left by the bulldozers when they'd thrown up the houses a year or so earlier. A bushy section of second-growth forest, a handful of maple trees, and some thin Douglas fir trees, bordered his property and that of the neighbor behind him. On Sunday mornings, the neighbor played Vivaldi, loud, and Mike Thomas stood on the balcony and shouted at him to turn it off.

Mom moved us in the summer. Mike Thomas had both our rooms stuffed with the things he'd brought to the house and never unpacked. His first wife had run a business out of one of the rooms, so it had chipped, pressboard desk, a plastic filing cabinet stuffed with blank paper, and Xerox boxes stuffed with blank forms. The rest of the house was furnished with temporary or portable furniture, folding chairs, card tables, bookcases made of fruit boxes, a ratty Persian carpet hiding a vomit stain of brown curry.

MY MOTHER, SICK OF MY FATHER constantly calling her, suggested he get together with Trudy. "She always had a thing for you." At this time, Trudy lived in Seattle where she worked as an operator for AT&T. She'd become pregnant by Mike McCree and he'd left her. She had a six-month-old son. When my father called her, she said, "Come right over."

My father and Trudy had sex. I could hear the sex coming up through the floorboards of the farmhouse. She screamed out the catalog a self-described screamer feels compelled to screech—"Bring it home baby," and "Oh yes," and "Drive it in, drive it in," and "Deeper and deeper!" She wanted us to hear. My father wanted us to hear. Their sex then in this little house was a way for my father to revenge himself on my mother.

My father observed while racing me to school one Monday morning, "Trudy is nine years younger than me. You're just eleven years younger than Trudy."

I looked out the window at a farmhouse in the middle of a field with a billboard facing Highway 18.

"I'm twenty years younger than you, Dad."

"She and you are practically the same age."

"She's eleven years older than me."

"She's pretty good looking."

I didn't know what to say to that, so I just nodded an indeterminate nod. Trudy stood almost a head taller than me and smelled of congealed nicotine and marijuana tar with a hint of strawberry that came from her all-natural shampoo.

"You could have sex with someone that was eleven years older than you."

I hoped he wasn't going where I thought he was going and I started to inform him that we were going to be late when he said it. "Would you like to have sex with Trudy?"

"No," I said.

"I mean you could. You could have sex with her."

"She's your girlfriend."

"We are engaged," Dad said. "She's going to be my wife."

"You're going to marry Trudy?"

"Yes I am. She's the best help mate I've ever had," he said.

We drove along then over the damp highway, the sound of crushed maple leaves squishing and the tires whirring on open patches of drizzle-slicked asphalt. My father often took the back roads. He had put this idea in my mind and I thought about sex with Trudy, my father's girlfriend, and while it didn't have any appeal at all, I couldn't stop thinking about the fact that he had a girlfriend rather than a wife who was my mother. It threw a different light on my father. Once I'd seen him as older and stronger. Now he seemed fragile and desperate.

DAD BURNED THINGS. He brought home old pallets from the back of warehouses, where they had written "free wood." He built gigantic bonfires in the middle of the field behind his house and burned everything he needed to get rid of. He burned discarded chests of drawers, splintered chairs, heaps of leaves, junk mail, and old newspapers. He sat near the flames that night and even though it was drizzling, he kept dry.

In the flickering dark, Dad began to talk about my mother, a long tirade, and at first my brother and I kept quiet, walking back away from the bright flames. My father and Trudy drank and threw their empty cans into the flames. My brother and I were foreign irritants, coming recently from my mother's house wearing new jackets and rolling our eyes as my father damped the tip of a joint with his tongue.

My mother, they said, had too high of an opinion of herself. She left my father to have an affair with a chinless limpdick. She didn't really care about us but really wanted to humiliate my father who really did love us and had always wanted the best for us. It didn't matter what they said, or that what they said didn't make any sense. And slowly, because it didn't seem to be quite real, our resolve not to say anything melted and my brother and I started saying things as well. We were angry with my mother, too. She could be the enemy. She could be the one who destroyed the way things had been. We all sat around the fire and howled and how fine we all felt.

In the morning, the fire pit smoldered in the rain with the charred remains of everything we had burned—white ash and twisted, seared blue bedsprings. When we went back to my mother's house, our new jackets smelling of hemp and wood smoke, Mom noticed our sullen responses about what we had done over the weekend. She knew we had dredged up every little detail of the new life she had forced on us all. We had told Dad and Trudy about the game hens she'd served on Tuesday night and her boyfriend's classical records, the dinner parties she threw with crystal vegetable dishes laid out with the cauliflower, broccoli, and carrots that nobody ate. She wondered if we hated her. Really we just hated having two families where we'd had one before. We hated being two different people, where before we could just be our parents' kids.

VERSIONS OF A STORY

Novella Mercedes Carpenter

WHEN ASKED TO EXPLAIN MY EXOTIC NAME to strangers at dinner parties, I shrug and say two words: *hippie parents*. That pronouncement made, in glides the ghost of hippie mythos—smelling of sandalwood, dressed in an embroidered shift, a joint in one hand, a baby in the other, and armed with big plans for living off the land. I should keep the photo of my mom wearing braids, bottle-feeding a calf, and looking utterly lost, in my purse for these occasions.

MY MOM, PATRICIA, sits in the shade of a walnut tree. It's early summer and I arrive, late and flustered from battling Seattle traffic, in my rusted-out Dodge Dart. As I pull up, I notice her car still has a peeling Beyond War sticker on the rear window, an artifact from her attempt in the eighties to make like-minded friends (proponents of world peace) in the sleepy logging town of Shelton, Washington. Only two other people showed up for the meeting. My mom never fit in Shelton, she was known as the divorcee, the single mother, the ex-hippie. She still wears her hair long, but the gray is pushing out the blonde at the temples. The few friends she's made indulge her and are willing to listen to her stories of Berkeley in the sixties.

She's been waiting for me—the lawn is mowed, and bread, cheese, and an uncorked bottle of wine are on the picnic table—but she acts casual, unconcerned. Iris, hardy geraniums, and bee balm spike out of carefully constructed mounds; raspberry canes and strawberries sprawl along the confines of a fragrant hedgerow; a small sedum garden nestles up around the koi pond. Strangers frequently peek over her garden gate to see what's growing. The cats, of which there are many, cluster outside her front door. She no longer allows them inside because they tear up the couch and—being all male and thus territorial—mark her couches and rugs with urine.

Sometimes, early in the summer, a few days after the Fourth of July, one can realize it's all over. A general feeling of things ending looms in all of that lushness. You look at the peas, and they're still flowering, but they'll never be as crisp and new as the ones before. My mom always tries to explain to me—and anyone else who will listen—that halcyon time before the peas of her youth started to wither. Her stories are glamorous and involve hanging out with Allen Ginsberg, being neighbors with Alice Waters, getting arrested protesting the Vietnam War. When she isn't telling stories, she hands out advice.

"Never marry a man you meet on vacation," she instructs, sighing into her chaise lounge, a fleet of cats at her fingertips. "It's suspended disbelief." When she says this she almost always launches into the story of how they met.

It was Berkeley, 1968, and the Bay Area hippie scene was being co-opted from every side. In late 1967, Pat had been walking down San Francisco's Haight Street, wearing a brown crocheted dress (with nothing underneath it) from the blow-out party the night before, when a bus screeched to a halt next to her. She heard the voice of the driver warble over a mike and hundreds of eyes peered at her from behind the glass. Pat was the first Genuine Hippie of that morning's tour. Her long hair swirled around her and she hurried out of view. The buzz was on: people wrote magazine articles about the hippies, and specials aired on television. San Francisco's streets and doorways glutted with young people who arrived just last week, en masse, to catch a piece of the famous free love and drugs. Pat was a carpetbagger herself—coming from upper-middle-class Southern California in the early sixties to study at UC Berkeley—but she had blended seamlessly into the youth movement, enthusiastically protesting the war, tilling up her apartment's parking strip to plant vegetables, and attending Grateful Dead shows at the Fil-more. The "new arrivals," as Pat called them, made these activities some-how less appealing, less underground. This is why Pat and her good friend Dixie spread an atlas out on Pat's yellow kitchen table and plot-ted their escape.

AFTER A COUPLE OF SUNNY MONTHS of cheap living, cultural mix-ups, and meaningless flings while driving down the Mexican coast, Pat and Dixie worked their way inland to San Miguel de Allende, a colonial city with cobblestone streets and a profusion of churches. Stepping out for dinner the first night there, Pat and Dixie encountered a dark-haired American playing classical guitar in the courtyard of their *posada*. He was from Portland, Oregon, and had been studying philosophy at Berke-ley before dropping out five credits short of graduation. He set his gui-tar down and they swapped travel stories. His name was George. He had studied French in Grenoble, knew carpentry, and liked to hunt and fish.

A Mexican family came into the courtyard and sold them a dinner of *tamales* followed by Chiclets. One of the children had a concertina, so George picked up his guitar and played along with the boy. The moon came up and the three Americans continued talking. Pat and Dixie both smoked steadily; an amorphous feeling of love hovered in the night air. Pat had a weakness for musicians—she always had been attracted to men with talents she didn't possess herself. It was understood that whichever one of the women went up to bed, the other would get to stay the night with George. Because Dixie had just had a fling with a local named Angel on the coast, she was the one who clomped up the clay steps back into the *posada*, and Pat claimed her prize. He seemed like a keeper. The wedding happened in a courtroom somewhere a few months later; the bride wore pants.

AFTER STINTS IN SPAIN AND FRANCE, the newlyweds returned to the States with the idea of going back to the land. Pat was anxious to start a family and suddenly the city that she had once loved seemed unnatural and crime-ridden. George convinced her to use her inheritance to buy a piece of land. And like so many other city-weary hippies, Pat and George headed to the country to try their hand at the simple life.

They chose Idaho. Pat yearned to grow peaches, perfect peaches, and the *Sunset Western Garden Book* had indicated that in Idaho she could do just that. The town of Orofino, surrounded by rolling hills with rocky outcroppings that erupted without warning, had reminded them of Spain's Costa Brava. The Clearwater River cut through the town, green and cold, carrying rainbow trout for George.

Hippies were oozing into the area from Moscow, Idaho (dropouts from U of I) to move back to the land, so there was a small sense of community to offset the friction that comes along with new blood in a small town. The hippies tried valiantly to blend in, using the word *howdy*, and stopping in the feed store to chat about the weather. Some succeeded only too well, and learned the local habit of sitting in dark bars for hours on end, and stowing a pistol in the glove box of their cars. In return, a few of the locals got turned on to a variety of psychedelic drugs.

Within that first year, Patricia gave birth to a daughter and found out that the *Sunset Western Garden Book* must have contained a typo—or in her haze of optimism she hadn't read the zone chart correctly—because it was way too cold to grow peaches in Orofino. The peach trees shriveled in her carefully constructed orchard, and didn't leaf out the following spring. She discovered that country living was nothing but hard work from dawn until dusk, and things went awry with regularity. As hard as she tried, she seemed not to be cut out for it. At the feed store, the lady behind the counter scowled at Pat's long, well-groomed fingernails, shook her head in disbelief, and said, "Honey, those nails are never gonna last." Pat had another daughter (the one thing she seemed good at) while George took to country life like a fish to water, going on weeklong elk-hunting trips on horseback, fraternizing with the locals, and pretending like he was Thoreau reincarnate.

I CAN COUNT ON MY FINGERS THE NUMBER of times I've seen my father since the divorce. The last time we met, he was in a hospital and I stepped into his room and said, "Hi, Dad." The man I spoke to, crumpled up in one of the beds, mutely pointed at the bathroom door like on a sitcom and then my dad appeared, balding but spry.

I've driven all the way to Idaho to see him, and we sit across the table from each other eating buffalo burgers. My dad has dribbled some sauce onto his chin. He's not supposed to eat burgers because of his cholesterol, but we just played a set of tennis (I won) and the waitress said they were good for us. I've driven all this way to get his side of the story, and he's trying to come off as guiltless as possible for the soured marriage: "I loved her, she loved me, we were living in an Eden. . . . But it was never enough for her."

Like my dad, my memories of their attempt to live off the land are pleasant, even idyllic: waking to George playing Bach's "Jesu, Joy of Man's Desiring" on a guitar he built himself; days spent eating fistfuls of strawberries with my sister; pagan dawn weddings followed by big outdoor pancake breakfasts; and treasure-hunt birthday parties with all the other hippie kids, where the big prize was hidden in the duck house by the pond.

George hasn't abandoned the living off the land philosophy. He reads Knut Hamson's *Pan* as a model for living. He still hunts and fishes for the majority of his food, shacks up in a little cabin in the Idaho hills. He claims he can witch water with a crooked stick. In him is a small grain of the need for comfort, though: he snowbirds it to Arizona every winter (he blames it on the frozen well, but we both know Idaho winters are too cold for an old man). There he practices guitar and plays tennis with the locals. People who don't know him often are charmed by his expansiveness, his obvious lust for life. Some people who do know him regard him as an asshole. He's stubborn, unconventional, not particularly well-mannered, and awfully hot tempered.

BECAUSE I WASN'T THERE, and my parents offer two different versions of the event that caused them to finally split, I can only speculate about what happened on that summer day.

The house we lived in on the ranch was called the Rough House, and it had few charms. I associate it with the color and smell of plywood—blonde, scratchy, never quite completely done. But Pat was adamant about its completion—wanting to lay red tile in the living room, insulate the walls, and finish the upstairs. So when George left for a weeklong logging expedition, she thought of Duward, the handyman who lived down the road.

Duward had escaped the East Coast and Cornell, intent on putting his skills as a carpenter to use in his everyday life. He knew friends of friends of Pat and George, who had a trailer on their ranch in Idaho and said that he could rent it for cheap. A man of few words, Duward occasionally walked down the rock and dirt road to their house for some coffee and a brief conversation about the weather. He had started work on a wooden boat out by the old goat house, steadily adding wood to a growing hull. He was working on the boat the day Pat walked down the road carrying a pitcher of lemonade and proposed that he help her finish building her house. There were bits of sawdust in his hair. He agreed.

There's a blurry photo of Duward in my mom's small photo album from the ranch days, nailing some stairs in an orange shirt and work boots. When I confront her with what my father has told me about Duward, she gets flustered. Unlike her other stories, where she is the hero, this is not one she wants to share.

It was midday and Duward had his shirt off. He was eating lunch by his truck when George returned from his adventures in the wilds. When he saw Duward, he flew into a rage. (My dad swears he could tell that Duward and Pat had been romantically involved.) He grabbed the first weapon he could find—a two-by-four—and charged. Duward pulled a gun from his glove box. As the men stood panting in the hot summer sun, the dust blowing a bit, Duward said in a low voice, "It's not worth killing a man over."

The men came to a truce, and no one was hurt. But Duward saw something in my dad's eyes—a wildness maybe—and packed his truck up for good, leaving the skeleton of his boat in the backyard.

"I remember that next morning standing on the porch of the Rough House, surveying everything," my mom says in the shade of the walnut tree, telling her version of the story (George was jealous, but nothing had transpired between her and Duward). "The goats had bleeding teats, you girls ran wild and ate dirt, the tomatoes and marigolds were mangled from a recent visit by a family of hungry deer. My partner, when he wasn't acting crazy, only did things his way—hunting when he wanted, ordering cattle we couldn't afford, logging trees off the property for money. Our house looked like a large version of a shack." She gestures to her yard and house, a Victorian cottage, "Maybe, when it came right down to it, all I wanted was a nice house." She sighs, "And I missed my old life."

Of course, those days were over. It was 1974, and things on communes, farms, and other experimental communities across the United States weren't working out as planned. It became clear to peace-loving hippies everywhere that the sixties' idealism had run dry, and the seventies—that decade of promise that some thought would be spent raising children and goats, spinning wool, and reinventing the word *community*—had become an era of messy divorces, nude sunbathing, and attending Eagles concerts in stadiums.

PERHAPS TO PROVE TO HERSELF that the places she remembers exist, Patricia goes back. Years ago, when I was in college, she invited me to go to San Blas, Mexico, one of the many beach towns she and Dixie visited before effectively finishing their trip in San Miguel de Allende.

I went because I was curious to see one of these places she waxed nostalgic over. We made an unlikely pair—my mom a middle-aged, slightly chubby matron; me a stick-legged sensitive type who, just before boarding the plane to Mexico, dyed my hair black and gave myself a spiky haircut. The dye smudged my neck and made for a strange suntan. I felt uncomfortable on this trip with my mother, as if I was supposed to be her Dixie. She donned a pair of extraordinarily long dangly turquoise earrings for the trip. When we rented our car at the airport, she elbowed me and insisted that I flirt with the counter boy. An awkward late bloomer at the time, I couldn't do it. "He was so cute," she murmured. "So cute. You have to make eye contact."

I had resigned myself to the fact that my future would never be as exciting, as daring as the past that she was always conjuring. When I planned a vacation to Spain she gave me advice about where to go even though she hasn't been back in thirty years. Her version of Europe involved months on a Greek island living with goat herders, more months in Paris, and a year in Spain spent picking grapes. My two-week trip was a drop of water next to an ocean.

We drove into the town of San Blas in a white rental car, and discovered that the whole town had been destroyed by a hurricane. We checked into a dreary room in the only hotel left standing. The town's one industry, advertised on cardboard signs everywhere—*pan de plantain* (banana bread)—had gone down with the high winds. Uprooted banana trees were scattered everywhere. A profusion of mosquitoes haunted us at night.

The beach the next day was cold and windy, but my mom convinced me to sit out anyway. She wore her hair down, and wrapped a batik shawl around her bathing suit. The beach's sand had clearly once been white, but now a resinous blackness clung to it, and garbage bobbed in the water. Every palm tree on the beach had been uprooted and hurled to far ends of the beach. You could see the outline of where a few thatched cabanas had once stood, ready to provide Cokes and coconuts and *pan de plantain*, but they too had blown away.

San Blas residents, understandably beaten down by their losses, glared at us from behind their poorly repaired shacks. Pat didn't notice this and got to telling the story of how she and Dixie had played volleyball on this very beach, and how they ate *chiles rellenos* in a restaurant painted bright turquoise on a dare from the local boys. "They were so hot, but we, the *gringas*, ate them!" she said, gazing out at the cloudy water. A fine, cold mist surrounded us, and I huddled under my beach towel listening, impatient for her to make a declaration about the past being over—clearly—amid this rubble.

Then it dawned on me. She did not see the destruction that surrounded us. Immersed in her memories of the freedom she'd had before her marriage, she hadn't noticed that the scene had shifted and left her behind. For a moment, I experienced the thrill of victory at seeing my mom so befuddled and so wrong. I admired the waves crashing against the dirty shore. Then a dread settled that has stuck with me. For the first time in my life up until then, I saw the inevitability of things going astray, of roads taken that led nowhere, of mistakes that can't be righted, of regret for what was but will never be again, until finally you are left with your own version of the story, and you cling to it like a castaway to a thin piece of wood.

Transitions

THE ENTROPY FACTOR

Alexandra Wolf

WHEN I WAS TWELVE I began having a recurring dream: I would be driving our huge two-tone Oldsmobile down a highway that dipped and curved through lush green hills. Of course, I didn't know how to drive back then, but in the dream it didn't matter—the car glided along of its own volition, hugging the road with a Porsche-like grace that utterly defied its sedan-ness. I'd relax against the brown velour as the Olds sped along, wind whipping my hair and sunlight glinting off the hood. It was exhilarating.

Then things would start to get weird. The car would start to pick up speed, and one by one the other cars would vanish into the distance behind me as quickly as windblown leaves in the rearview mirror. The scenery would shift abruptly to a seasonless desert of blanched grays and browns. Suddenly I would realize that I had no idea how to drive; I was just a twelve-year-old from Manhattan—what did I know about cars? What the hell was I doing?

I would grope for the brakes, but I didn't even know where to look for them, and nothing seemed to work. The Olds would continue accelerating, menacing groans now issuing from the engine. The dashboard looked like a maze of dials and blinking lights more appropriate to a 747 than an '81 Cutlass, and I had no clue what anything was for. Panic would begin welling up, but luckily the road led off in a perfectly straight line toward infinity. There was nothing to hit. I just had to figure out how to stop the car.

Then the wall would appear. Solid brick. Straight across the horizon. Adrenaline would surge through my body as I frantically twiddled knobs and pushed buttons trying to find the brakes. In the end, I would hunch forward and cling to the steering wheel, watching the wall lurch toward me until I was so close I could see the grain of the brick. Then I'd wake up.

This went on for about two weeks straight. Then I began dreaming that my mother was driving the car and that I was the passenger. I would scream helplessly, but she'd never acknowledge my presence. I seemed to be invisible and mute like a ghost riding next to her. I would wake up panting and drenched in sweat.

When my mother offered to take me shopping one day in the midst of all this, I declined. I was feeling strange and uncertain. I didn't want to go with her. I didn't want to see my friends. Instead I stayed home with my brother, David, and my grandmother, who was visiting us from California. I spent the afternoon fluttering around the apartment, nervously pestering Grandma about Mom's whereabouts. The phone call came in the late afternoon: Mom had crashed the car, and she was in the hospital.

It turned out that she had hit a concrete median and flipped the car completely. Her arm had flown out the open window and the car rolled over on it, crushing her hand. The Olds was totaled—the roof was embedded in the seat on the passenger side and caved in across the entire backseat, leaving only a small bubble of safety around where my mother had been sitting. It was miraculous that she survived. Anyone else in the car would certainly have been dead.

When we arrived at the hospital, my father was already there, looking shaken, but Mom seemed coherent and upbeat, joking about how she'd never do another Palmolive commercial, but that she was basically okay. Her hand was bandaged up and we couldn't see how bad it looked, but she assured us that somehow nothing had even broken, and the doctors believed she would make a nearly full recovery. As we were leaving, a nurse ran up to us holding out a pink plastic cup.

"Don't forget this," she said and handed it to my mother, who in turn handed it to me. I looked down and saw two slightly mangled gold crescents.

"My finger was all smushed, so they had to saw off my wedding ring," she said. "Hang onto that for me."

Shortly afterward, my parents sat David and me down to tell us they were getting divorced.

I never knew exactly why my mother left my father. My parents were not big fighters—if they were arguing a lot, they kept it behind closed doors. David, who was nine at the time, was so blissfully unaware that when they called us in for the big talk, he thought they were going to announce that we were getting a canoe. I knew something was amiss, but I've always felt that the question was better left unasked. What I do know is that my mother's near-death experience catapulted her into the decision that she needed something more out of life—and whatever she was looking for wasn't within our family.

I grew up at an unlikely intersection of several different social spheres. We lived in Inwood, a working-class Irish-American neighborhood at the northern tip of Manhattan, which was a lot like a small town. It was completely safe, and everyone knew everyone, yet we had access to all Manhattan had to offer. My parents would take my brother and me to museums and performances, but we were also able to play unsupervised in the park, and I spent much of my childhood climbing trees, skateboarding down rain gutters, and inventing new and complicated versions of tag with the neighborhood kids.

I had plenty of friends, but I never exactly fit in. My parents are both highly educated people who went around saying things like, "It is I," yet we lived in a world of "dese, dems, and dose." My father's colorful New York Jewish accent warred with my mother's perfect Midwestern anchorwomanese—and my brother and I ended up with a hybrid sound that defies geography and confuses everyone. I heard the term "fake" batted around more than once. We were also the only Jewish kids in our largely Catholic community. I was asked if my horns had been removed at birth, branded a "rich bitch," and reprimanded for being a member of the group that killed Jesus. Once I was chased by an angry mob of rock-hurling prepubescents led by an acid-wash-clad Naziette who kept yelling, "Get the kike!"

Even with my closest friends, the whole religion issue could be very alienating. My best friend Caroline had a beach house, and whenever we went out there, I'd go to church with her and her mother. I was always intimidated. I didn't understand anything. And this particular church had an enormous and especially gory Christ hanging above the pulpit. I knew he was supposed to be a good guy, but the image disturbed me nonetheless. I would sit there trying not to look at it, and aping whatever Caroline did. When she stood, I stood. When she kneeled, I kneeled. I even took a stab at mumbling some prayers along with everyone else. One day we went to mass just after Caroline had started taking communion. When she got in line, I filed in right behind her. I had no idea what we were doing. When I got to the front of the line, I was offered the wafer and wine. I heard the priest say "Body of Christ, blood of Christ." I stopped dead in my tracks and asked, "Really?" The priest was appalled.

"Of course, really!" he exclaimed.

"I'm not eating that!" I said, looking around at the other people in line like they were crazy. The terrible truth had been revealed: These were a bunch of cannibals who worshipped a dead guy on a stick. And now I was supposed to take a nibble of this Christsicle just to fit in? I was having none of it. Several people chimed in with commentary, and I began to freak out. By now Caroline's mother had already gone through the line, but she turned around to see what all the commotion was about, and then came to the rescue.

"I'm so sorry, Father," she said, looking embarrassed. "She's Jewish," she explained, as if this accounted for any number of flaws I might have.

I never really felt Jewish except in moments like that. My mother isn't Jewish, and my father was never especially big on ceremonies. We celebrated both Christmas and Chanukah. We had a Passover Seder, and we went to synagogue twice a year for the High Holidays, but I never considered religion to be a very big part of my life.

Ironically, at school I often felt that I wasn't Jewish enough. I had a scholarship to Riverdale Country School, a very exclusive private school where most of the students were wealthy Jewish kids—but I didn't seem to have much in common with them either. I didn't have big curly hair like all the other girls. I lived in the wrong neighborhood. I had the wrong accent and the wrong clothes. My parents scoffed at the idea of buying me the Benetton sweaters and Guess? jeans that would have helped me blend in there, but in retrospect, I would have stood out as a geek even with them. I made friends with the less snobby girls, but I always felt like a bit of a novelty act.

By the time I was in junior high, I began to feel like a freak. I was neither here nor there. And it was all because my parents were oddballs from another dimension—one where TV was limited to an hour per week; where adult members of the household wandered the apartment in their underwear; where hankies were used instead of Kleenex in order to save the trees. I was embarrassed that they had taken pictures of me and David dancing naked in the woods. I didn't understand the well-meaning social experiment they were conducting when they insisted on non-branded, gender-neutral toys. I failed to see the health benefits of being denied Cap'n Crunch or limiting my exposure to *The Dukes of Hazzard*. There seemed to be no end to the bizarre ideas that issued from their wheatgerm-addled minds. But they weren't simply a couple of hippies either—they weren't even hip. Dad listened exclusively to classical music, and Mom liked to drop casual references to Greek and Roman history into everyday conversations. There was no getting around it—they were weirdos and I was doomed to turn out weird as a result —yet despite all my misgivings, I also knew that the one place I felt truly at home was with my family.

We lived in a big messy apartment awash in fur from our various dogs, cats, and other assorted pets. Both of my parents worked from home at various points, so there was always someone around. Dad would be there hunched over his contact sheets with a magnifying glass or Mom would be sitting in her multicolored office marking up manuscripts with a red pen. The living room was encircled with overflowing bookcases that gave off a certain leathery smell I'll always associate with my childhood. And the whole house was littered with mementos from various projects and experiments, like Mom's huge, perpetually half-finished papier-mâché elephant or my collection of baby teeth sitting in glasses of different kinds of soda to see which rotted first. Dinner was a raucous event where everyone talked at once and anything went. David once began telling us a dead serious story that opened with, "Once, when I was a dog. . . ." We made up our own words and our own games. Our sport of choice was dueling with empty plastic two-liter Coke bottles. It sounds corny even now, but that little universe was truly the one place I never felt like I had to explain who I was. But after the divorce, it all disintegrated—it simply couldn't exist without all four of us in the mixture.

There was some fighting over property, but thankfully my parents agreed on joint custody of David and me from the start, and they both made a real effort not to badmouth each other. My mother moved out into a two-bedroom apartment in an adjacent neighborhood, and we were to alternate—one week with Dad, one with Mom. They tried to make us comfortable with the new arrangement. They even spoiled me a little for the first time in my life. David and I had always shared a bedroom growing up, but now I had my own room in both places, and I was given free reign to decorate as I chose. I inherited my mom's former office, which I decorated in an ultra-stark mod theme in black and white. I couldn't believe Dad actually consented to getting me custom-made black blinds and my own sleek white telephone. Mom also bent over backwards, giving David and me the two bedrooms at her house, while she slept on a pullout couch in the living room. There I opted for a dried-roses-on-the-wall, thrift store candelabra look. It was everything my childhood persona was not. I remember feeling very grown-up in my new private shrines to girldom. I tossed my tomboy routine, and decided that I was no longer a child—I was a little adult who just happened to live with her parents.

I had always been a straight-A student and a generally well-behaved child, but suddenly I began to slide. I would probably have been a rebellious teenager whether my parents had remained married or not, but the split certainly turned up the volume. Back when they were married, my parents posed a united front on discipline issues. Once they were apart, Dad turned into a white-knuckled rule junkie, and Mom dissolved into a total marshmallow. It was a situation ripe for disaster. Residual threads of filial respect had a tenuous hold on me at first, but that didn't last long. It was easy to reject my parents when our family as I knew it had just evaporated. I didn't even feel like I was rejecting anything—it just seemed like the childhood chapter of my life was over, and with it went everything holding me back.

Right after the divorce my father began scrutinizing me more closely than ever. He'd ask me where I went when I took the dog for a walk, and then he'd accuse me of lying because I failed to mention that I stopped at the deli on the way. He would grill me about every moment I spent with friends, and act offended or suspicious when I told him we were just hanging out. I would be locked in the bathroom extracting pepperoni from my braces or maiming my hair with a curling iron, and he'd start pounding on the door, demanding to know what on earth I was doing in there. I felt like I was under a microscope, and I resented being treated like a criminal when I wasn't even doing anything wrong.

After eighth grade I transferred to Bronx Science, a public high school, where I suddenly went from being the "scholarship kid" to being one of the cool kids. I discovered that boys liked me. I started cutting classes to smoke pot with the burnouts or wander Manhattan in the daytime when we felt like we had the whole city to ourselves. I bought a black leather jacket and punched seven holes in my ears using a potato and a safety pin. My biggest problem in life was my 9:00 P.M. curfew. I begged my father to give me a little leeway, but he refused to budge an inch, so I began lying to him about my whereabouts—telling him I was sleeping over at friends' houses so that I could go to parties and nightclubs. He always seemed to think I was up to no good anyway, I figured I might as well. So I ended up staying out all night, and since I knew I wouldn't be coming home, there was no point in staying sober either.

Meanwhile, Mom's house was a parentless paradise where David and I ate pizza for dinner and did as we pleased. My mother was out dating all the time, and I was perfectly content with the fact that she barely seemed to notice what I was up to. Even when she was there, it hardly mattered—I had a lock on my door and a fire escape at my bedroom window. I would tell her I was going to bed, and then I'd sneak out the window. I'd meet up with my girlfriends and we'd down a fifth of Jack Daniels in the park. Then we'd head out to the club of the moment and dance all night in our cut-offs and bustiers. When the sun came up we'd usually go out for cheese fries at a trendy all-night diner called The Coffee Shop, but occasionally things went awry. Once I lost my friends at the Limelight and ended up leaving with three guys I had met that night. We went up to the Bronx and broke into some mansion's private grounds where we proceeded to go skinny-dipping. They were all in their twenties, and I remember thinking it was hilarious that they had no idea how old I was. When I finally made them guess that I was only fourteen, they hastily put their clothes back on and took me out for pancakes instead of whatever else they had been planning. I was lucky that time.

Things came to a head when I began seeing a Columbia student named Paul. He was twenty, I was fifteen. We were bonded at the hip right from the beginning. I saw nothing wrong with our age gap. I simply took it as further testimony to my own maturity, but my father was quite rightly disturbed. Although he never outright forbade me from seeing Paul, he did everything he could to discourage it. Unfortunately, he had taught me to question authority, and that's exactly what I did. I didn't care what he thought of my relationship, and there wasn't really any way to punish me. I was too headstrong to be grounded and I had plenty of money from working as a lifeguard, so allowance was not a bargaining tool. There was simply no way to stop me.

When I stayed at my mother's, I would sneak Paul in through my fire escape at night. When I stayed with my father, I had to wait until the weekends, and then I would tell him I was staying at a girlfriend's house. I'm sure they were both onto me, but my mother chose to look the other way. Perhaps she recognized that creepy as it was, Paul was actually keeping me out of more trouble than he was getting me into. But Dad wasn't about to let it fly, and he met me head-on.

One night I was staying at Paul's, and Dad called up in the middle of the night. For some reason I answered the phone. Dad went ballistic. He was shouting at me to get in a taxi right that minute and come home. I refused. He insisted that if I couldn't live by his rules, then I couldn't live under his roof. At that point I uttered the most shameful thing I think I've ever said. I told him that I could fuck Paul at two in the afternoon if I wanted, so what difference did it make? I said, "What are you going to do? Lock me in a tower?" Needless to say, he kicked me out, and we didn't speak for more than a year. From that point on I was exiled to Mom's domain.

When David stayed with Dad, I had the house almost all to myself, and I lived more like a college freshman than a high school girl. Paul stayed over more and more. I had a job as a lifeguard. I became a club kid and I cut school regularly, although somehow I managed to stay on the swim team and avoid flunking out. I did my own cooking (Burger King) and my own housework (none). When David was around, I was on slightly better behavior so as not to upset him. He had become a sulky, angry little kid who seemed to hate me for no good reason. Despite the fact that I was busily rejecting just about everything, I had always thought we were on the same team. But suddenly he would barely even talk to me. He would come in and throw his backpack on the floor, then sit there playing Atari with a vacant stare or stomp around the house slamming doors. He always seemed to be on the brink of an outburst, and for a long time, he insisted on calling me "Slut" or "Druggie" even though I couldn't imagine that he knew much about what I was actually doing.

One day I was home alone with Paul, and we were in my bedroom fooling around. I usually locked my door, but I wasn't expecting anyone to be home, and I hadn't bothered. Suddenly the door burst open and David popped in, completely oblivious to the fact that we were there. I was on all fours in nothing but a bra and panties. David barged halfway into the room before he noticed us. I froze, my mouth still full of cock, and our eyes locked for a nauseating instant. His jaw dropped almost as wide as mine. Then he bolted out of the room.

For days we avoided each other. We couldn't even make eye contact. One night Mom made us dinner, and the three us of sat at the table in near silence the whole time—a historical event in my family. Mom demanded to know what was wrong, but neither of us would utter a word. Late that night, I was making myself a snack when David came into the kitchen and sheepishly approached me.

"I just wanted you to know that I didn't see anything the other day," he said. It was an absurd lie, but I appreciated the effort.

"Oh, right!" I said, laughing, and for some reason I flung my yogurt or whatever it was at him. Next thing I knew, we were both laughing hysterically and having a huge food fight. It was the first time we had actually laughed together in what seemed like years. The noise must have woken my mother up, and she suddenly materialized in her nightgown, again demanding explanations for our increasingly strange behavior. We never told her a thing, but now at least it felt more like an inside joke than an unspeakable trauma.

Things were slightly better between the two of us after that, but we were still pretty estranged all through my high school years. After that I left for college, and by the time I graduated, he was just starting, so we barely saw each other for most of a decade. It's only been in the past few years that he and I have really started to become close. He recently told me that during those first few years after the split, he was convinced that my mother and I were always trying to give him the slip. He said that every time we took a trip anywhere, he dreaded whenever the two of us disappeared into the women's bathroom, fearing that it was really a secret way out, and that we were never coming back. That nearly broke my heart.

These days he and I share more of a common perspective on our parents. We spend a lot of our time together fretting over their well-being in a premature parent/child role reversal. Our mother has completely reinvented herself to conform to her boyfriend's ideals, and we both find her hard to relate to sometimes. Our father is remarried to an extremely difficult woman, who has caused more than her share of strife for everyone. We are actually fairly close to both our parents, but there is no sense of any larger "family." Both of them have been wholly consumed by their respective significant others, and our relationships seem to float in some totally disconnected realm. I see each of the three members of my family on a regular basis, but it is often a one-on-one affair. We chat about our lives and interests against an ever-changing backdrop of restaurants and parks, museums and cafes. There are no big family events; there is no comfy old house crammed with childhood mementos, no sense of continuity. They are not truly involved in my life nor I in theirs. We merely seem to give each other updates on what's going on as if we were old friends who live in different cities.

Most of the time, I'm content with this arrangement. But there are times when that sense of rootlessness can be painful. I have grown to dread the holidays, because there's nowhere to go that I feel comfortable. Both of my parents celebrate all the holidays exclusively with their new families. The last time I had Thanksgiving with any of my blood relatives was three years ago. That year David was away, and Mom took me to dinner at her boyfriend's sister's house. I naturally assumed that her boyfriend would be there, but it turned out that he couldn't even attend, so it was just the two of us. Mom assured me that they were very nice people and that I would enjoy myself even though I didn't know them well. We drove out to their house in New Jersey, homemade pumpkin pies in tow. When we arrived, they warmly ushered us in past the lawn gnomes to a cozy basement room. I surveyed the '70s style paneling, the sweet potato ambrosia, and thought: This is all harmless enough. But it quickly became clear that everyone there had already been briefed on my political views as well as a number of details about my personal life— and the head of that household apparently had issues with many of them. He started off with some gentle ribbing ("So they tell me you're a big tree-hugger"), and I laughed along, but refused to take the bait. As the meal wore on, he began escalating into a full-scale personal assault. I tried to change the topic, but he wouldn't be deterred. Some of his lead-ins sounded rehearsed. I had the feeling he had been saving up for me as if this were some kind of Thanksgiving pageant entertainment. Look, kids! A real live left-winger. Watch Grandpa torture her with his inanities. Meanwhile, Mom sat there mutely downing turkey. I finally shot her a say-something look, at which point she excused herself to the bathroom for the next half hour or so. When she finally emerged, I cornered her in the kitchen and requested that we wrap things up as soon as possible, since we were stranded in the middle of nowhere and I couldn't just walk out and hail a cab. We were there for another six hours. Since then I've hosted "Orphans' Thanksgiving" at my house, and there's always a good turnout of New York transplants who couldn't make it back to the folks in Wichita.

An even uglier scenario arose last fall when my father had surgery on his spine. He developed some post-op complications that ultimately healed, but for a few days it looked like he might never walk again. He was terrified and in excruciating pain. Apparently this was not reason enough for my father's wife to put her differences with me aside and try to help him as best she could. Instead she tried to bar me from seeing him, despite the fact that he was begging me to come and take care of him. I insisted on coming over anyway, of course, and in retaliation, she actually tried to throw my father out of the house in the middle of the night when he couldn't even stand. In short, she made an already stressful situation completely unbearable for everyone involved. I guess things like that happen even among blood relatives, but I can't imagine either of my parents ever behaving that way, and it's at times like that when I can't help wondering how things might have been different if they had stayed together.

I can't deny that the divorce has deeply affected my life. However, I've never seen myself as a victim nor do I view divorce as a tragedy. I just accepted it as an immutable fact of my life like growing up in New York or being born with a certain IQ. There were certain unpleasantries associated with it, but I can't say that they were any worse than things that happen in any other family—particularly ones with bad marriages at their heart. I never saw the divorce itself as a direct cause of any of my problems. My brother once told me that he has always envisioned a parallel version of himself—the person he might be if our parents had stayed married. I realized that I had never second-guessed the issue. I've often wondered if my parents themselves might have been better off, but I can't imagine myself out of that context. I am who I am.

Recently I ended a very long-term relationship. When I told my parents, both of them responded with different versions of an "I'm sorry it didn't work out" theme, with its underlying implication that marriage had been the ultimate goal. When I told them that I'm not sorry, and that I'm in no hurry to get married, especially since I'm fairly certain I don't want children, they were both deeply dismayed. My father said he thought the divorce had damaged me. I tried to explain that I don't feel damaged—I simply have a different point of view. I just don't buy into the idea that settling down and raising children is the best choice for everyone. Perhaps my sense of the ephemeral nature of relationships can be traced to the divorce, but is that necessarily damage? Maybe I've just been liberated from certain outdated and unrealistic expectations. I may be skeptical of the idea of "forever," but I'm not a true cynic—I'm quite capable of falling hopelessly in love. I just have a keener understanding than most that things don't always go according to plan, so I try not to get too wrapped up in the future. After all, divorce is proof that life is unpredictable.

WHEREVER YOU WANT

Douglas Goetsch

WHEN I SAID FUCK YOU TO MY FATHER for not paying child support like the judge ordered, we were at his bachelor pad in Smithtown, in a wing of a house that looked out on a backyard swimming pool where somebody's kids were playing. He offered me a ride home, but I slammed the door and started walking. When he drove up alongside me I gave him the finger, held it up like a torch, until he finally peeled away, leaving me alone for the walk. Ten miles. I liked it.

I WENT ON WALKS ALL SUMMER, out Elwood Road past my high school, past the next town's high school, walking the shoulder at dusk, headlights streaking across my eyes as I tried for perfect steps, absorbing shocks with my ankles, knees, hips, so that my head floated on top of me as though dangling from the heavens by a silk thread. I walked Jericho Turnpike, miles of car dealers, furniture showrooms, funeral homes, strip malls, broken glass. I stopped at the sign for The Tender Trap, the letters pink and black, tall as me. I'd passed it hundreds of times in the car with Mom.

THE FAT GUY AT THE DOOR didn't even card me, just took my three bucks and said, "Enjoy yourself, son." I stepped through a curtain of black rubber slats like you find in a car wash. A woman was kneeling on the bar, circling her hips in the face of a bald guy who looked like Mr. Damuelowitz, my Little League coach. I took a seat at the other end. I tried to signal the bartender to order a drink. Instead, the stripper— though not *technically* a stripper because she had no clothes to take off—got up and headed over, cellulite jiggling on her legs, men lifting their heads sheepishly as she passed. She stopped in front of me, crouched down, opened her thighs, rocked her torso forward and back, forward and back like a nauseating reflection in a doorknob. She smelled a little rubbery, a little like Mom, breasts pointing down at me like tired accusations.

ANOTHER TIME I KICKED A BOTTLE CAP down 25A, which banked around hills by the harbor, then turned inland at the Charcoal Cottage, where Mom had passed out the year before after two sips of a Southern Comfort sour. Dad told everyone to just let her lie there until she came to. But I threatened the manager, who called the paramedics, who swore Mom had the lowest blood pressure on record. We watched them work on her, then strap her onto a gurney and drive off. A year later Dad left in the night. His train station car, the Gremlin, with all those blue *New York Times* delivery bags in the back, became his getaway car. He drove to the Commack Motor Inn for his rendezvous with Mrs. Kaufman, and they each phoned to call off their marriages. Next day at noon Dad drove up in the Gremlin. He'd come for the pictures of ships in his study, marching back and forth through the bedroom, where Mom still had the covers over her head, swearing she'd lie there until she died.

I'D BEEN KICKING THE SAME BOTTLE CAP FOR MILES, through Northport, Centerport, Greenlawn, into Huntington, where the Galaxy Diner sat wrapped like a birthday present in shining chrome, its neon sign blazing "OPEN ALL NIGHT." I gazed at the cakes and pies in the revolving case, the toppings piled high and stiff like the old waitress's hair. "Wherever you want," she said. I was the only customer. I sank into a cushioned booth and ordered coffee and lemon meringue pie. Mom could make about three things well, and lemon meringue pie was one of them. I used to stand on a chair next to her as she gently tossed the yolks from shell to shell over a glass bowl. Just the littlest bit of yolk, she said, would contaminate the whites and they would never rise. She poured in sugar, a teaspoon of vanilla, and got out the mixer. I watched the amber puddle climb the sides of the bowl, turning pure white—how could so much come from so little, I wondered. She spread the meringue thick over lemon filling, making peaks and tufts with the edge of the spatula, which I would soon get to lick. In the Galaxy Diner, miles from home, I spackled each forkful of pie onto the roof of my mouth, licked it down, let some of it turn to juice, smeared the rest back up again, and again, until it all dissolved.

THREE-WAY

Peppur Chambers

WHENEVER I ENTER A DRY CLEANER, I'm reminded of Texas. My mother worked as a cashier in one when I was eleven. After school, my two younger brothers and I would walk to the store and wait for her until she was done working. We'd arrive dusty, thirsty, and hungry to be greeted by my tired mother's smiling face. She'd kiss us on the forehead and quickly send us off to our corner in the back where we'd quietly do our homework. Participating in the "I'll pick up the kids Tuesday, you pick them up Wednesday" carpool with other mothers wasn't an option for *her*.

The chemical-scented warmth powered by the steam of the pressing irons in the back enveloped and suffocated me at the same time. I hated being confined, regulated to one area, and told to be quiet. It felt as if my mouth was bound with an invisible strip of duct tape. Occasionally, I would sneak to the far back past the racks of clothes draped in plastic to run my hand along the smooth, scorched pressing pad and feel the weight of the heavy metal handle, as I pretended to rejuvenate a customer's party dress or white starched shirt. I somehow found comfort in the pressing pad's powerful strength. Never straying for long, I'd return to my corner lassoed by feelings of responsibility. As an adult, that rope has never left my neck.

As the oldest child I was saddled with unwanted intuition. I knew my mother needed this dry-cleaning job. She needed the money. We needed the money. This wasn't a side gig where part of her hard-earned dollars became a weekly allowance to us for walking the dog or a check attached to a permission slip for a class trip to the zoo. This was money that bought the Wonder Bread and grape jelly that became our lunch: lone grape jelly sandwiches that were never a hot commodity for the daily food-trade in the school cafeteria. "A grape jelly sandwich?!" my schoolmates would exclaim in their disapproving southern twang. I could never defend nor hype why they should want a grape jelly sandwich in exchange for Fritos or their beloved okra.

At the end of Mom's shift, we'd walk home to our apartment complex. It was complex in more ways than one. We had moved to Texas for a better life. My blood sister—a true cut-your-finger-smoosh-blood blood sister—and her mother (my mom's party neighbor and absolute friend for life) had made the pilgrimage to Texas years before. Letters and phone calls to us in Wisconsin spoke of warm weather and plentiful jobs. Soon, invitations to visit were replaced with enticements for us to move there as well.

So in 1981, with dreams of prosperity, my recently divorced, twenty-nine-year-old mother left the comfort of our three-bedroom flat, friends, family, and familiarity and drove us, along with the man who would become our new stepfather, to Dallas, Texas. We left everything behind: the furniture; the huge stereo I played my Doobie Brothers' album on; my cat, Sylvester; my three-year old philodendron. We took only what could fit in our used Sierra Vista station wagon. If there were a country song about peein' in cups and eatin' biscuits 'n' gravy at truck stops, that would have been the anthem for our cross-country trek.

We stayed with my blood sister and her mother in Dallas until we found our own place in Arlington, Texas. The moment our caravan rolled into the new parking lot, my brothers and I spotted our first fortune. A pool. We had our very own pool. Mom let us go swimming as fast as we could unpack and wiggle into our swimming suits. We had all taken lessons and my brothers were fearless on the diving board. As I took a break on a lounge chair by the side of the pool, a beautiful lime-green and yellow butterfly landed on my one-piece swimsuit. It unrolled its tongue and sipped a droplet of sunkissed water.

WHEN WE MOVED FROM WISCONSIN, Mom thought it was best not to tell our dad we were leaving (I assume that their custody agreement had borders and maybe she wanted to live without them). We lived in a charade for a while before the move, and then one day we were gone. I can't imagine how my father must have felt driving up to our vacant house, walking up to our wooden porch, then staring in panicked disbelief through curtainless windows at an empty living room. What did he do when the truth sank in? How do you react when you're thirty-three years old and your ex-wife has kidnapped your children?

Once we arrived in Texas, it was my job to call my father weekly from a pay phone outside the A&P grocery store while my brothers roamed the aisles and my lanky, John Lennon–esque stepfather stole meat for our dinner:

"Hi, Dad."

"Where are you, baby?" he'd ask.

"We're okay. We love you," I'd reply with my mother coaching in the background: "Do *not* tell him where we are."

"Just tell me where you are," he'd plead.

"I have to go now. Bye."

I was ten years old.

Eventually, my mother made her own phone call and disclosed our whereabouts to him. That conversation resembled all the others they'd had since the divorce: screaming, cursing, not listening; only this time she was in front of the A&P and people were staring—first in amazement at the sailor-mouthed ferociousness of this 5′1″ black woman and then with pity at me. As kids with divorced parents, not only were we required to grow up quickly, but we were also forced to watch our parents act like idiots.

My parents divorced when I was eight. (That phrase, "My parents divorced . . ." is a tape-recorded mantra that every child of divorce recites; it's embedded in our minds like "I pledge allegiance . . ."). Because I was so young, I don't have many memories of us living as a happy, conventional family. In fact, we lived somewhat unconventionally. My father was a resident advisor (RA) at a local Lutheran college and we lived in the designated RA apartment, which was in the dorm. My brothers and I were raised by a village of white college kids, until they would call my mother to come and get us out of their dorm rooms. Life was fun then, because I was a kid and we were together; and, I suppose, I didn't know any better. Neither did my parents.

We were a young family. Dad was twenty-one when he married my eighteen-year-old pregnant mother and my brothers quickly followed over the next six years. (I can't imagine having three kids before the age of thirty; I can barely take care of my plants.) My parents got married because of me. Sometimes I think, "Hey! *I* started this," and I feel very powerful. Other times I just thank God I'm alive, because some people never make it out of the box.

Mom and Dad met in Great Falls, Montana, while he and my mom's father were stationed at the air force base there. Mom's family and my dad were just about the only black folks in town, so there may not have been much for my tall chocolate-brown basketball-playing daddy and my former cheerleading café-au-lait mommy to choose from in terms of dating. However fate was working, I'm glad they chose each other. I've always said that I'm destined to be great because I was born in *Great* Falls. We stayed in Montana a year before moving on to Indiana and finally Wisconsin, where Dad had received a basketball scholarship to one of the universities. He had wanted to play hoops professionally, and followed that dream until impending responsibility and my grandma's (his mother's) stern disapproval stopped him.

Youth, unfulfilled dreams, ego, 1970s black power, and feminism were just a few reasons that probably contributed to my parents' divorce, which my father did not want. But, does it really matter *why* they divorced? All that really matters is that twenty-two years later, I'm blessed to have loving and respectful relationships with my father, mother, and stepmother; and have a titanium bond with my two brothers. Sure, I'll never be able to hand down my parents' wedding rings to my children (Dad threw his in Lake Michigan and Mom pawned hers for a can of tuna, a box of Kraft macaroni and cheese and two packages of hot dogs), but what are materialistic family heirlooms when you've got love and their baggage to pass on?

IN TEXAS, OUR LITTLE POT OF GOLD may as well have been watered-down molasses. Life was rich with love and emotion but barren in every other respect. After a while, we had lots of laughs but no money. My mother and stepfather's art hung on the walls, but we had no furniture. My room was furnished with a wooden pallet that was my bed. It was padded with a thick, beautiful Pakistani wool blanket my grandfather had given to me. My mother, always the creative optimist, would say it was like an Asian futon.

"This type of bed is very good for your back," she told me, ending her informative talk with, "Isn't this fun?"

I thought so until my *only* friend came for a visit and I had trouble answering questions regarding the absence of living-room furniture and explaining the fun in sleeping on a discarded crate and a blanket. In Wisconsin, I'd had a fabulous four-poster cherrywood bed. Sometimes I would attach some heavy string to a deflated rubber bouncy ball and tie it to the bedpost and we would play tetherball in my bedroom. Now *that* was fun.

If payback is a bitch, irony is a motherfucker. That winter, Arlington was hit with a record-breaking blizzard—we even went ice skating in the parking lot. Our family had escaped from Wisconsin only to be bombarded with all the things we were trying to get away from. We stayed there for six months then returned to Wisconsin with more of the nothing we left with. Life changed again when my mother came to the desperately insightful conclusion that maybe my father could provide a better home for us and decided to give him full custody.

I PLEADED WITH MY MOTHER not to send us to my father. My dad
didn't know how to make a futon out of a wood crate. He didn't know
how to braid my hair. He didn't sing and dance in the living room. And,
he didn't call me *chickenlicken*. I was certain there had to be another
alternative; but I knew by the defeat in my mother's eyes that there was
none. I was *very* disappointed. She and I had become a team that fought
hardships with laughter, took care of my brothers, and battled my dad.
We'd formed a mother–daughter bond that should not have been broken. In the process, Dad had been dissed—often. I loved him, but her
seeds of dissension had already been planted and they were soon sprout-
ing weeds in me.

The monumental return to my father was planned without his permission or knowledge. (It's easier to become a master magician of the
"now you see them, now you don't" trick when you perform it without
forewarning.) One day we appeared at Dad and his fiancée's one-
bedroom apartment, just as they were starting a life together. *Surprise.*

Understandably, my father was not amused. When we arrived, I was
so tall and skinny that I looked like a scarecrow; and my brothers were
wearing yellow sleeveless puffy vests on which they had scrawled in
bleeding red Magic Marker "WARRIORS!" in cool likeness of the gang
from the movie of the same name. These vests had been Dad's Christmas present to them the year before. We felt pretty normal, but he stared
at us in shock, probably wondering what the hell he was going to do
with us.

My mother's trick cost us, and for the next seven years, she paid. No
visitation, phone calls, or letters. We barely saw or spoke to her from the
time I was in sixth grade until I graduated college. This was partially due
to her second survival tactic. After she left us, she and my stepfather
enlisted in the army, with its nifty free room and board. Near the end of
her duty, she was stationed in Mannheim, Germany, for several months,
and liked Germany so much that she ended up staying there two years.
We, of course, didn't have passports.

My dad came to the rescue and moved us into a three-bedroom
apartment. We welcomed mattressed beds, clothing, and a well-stocked

refrigerator. Dad let us know that we would never have to worry about anything ever again. But we were really a bunch of strangers living under the same roof pretending to be a family. Aside from not having physically seen us for the previous six months, Dad had only seen us weekly from 1978 to 1980 in accordance with his court-appointed visitation rights. My brothers had to reacquaint themselves with their own father; I already thought he was my enemy and didn't want to know him. We didn't know his fiancée—I think we'd seen each other maybe three times up to that point. Further, she and Dad were diving into the unknown by living together for the first time.

We lived with a rolling tension that loomed above our heads like a dark sky. There were some difficulties in the beginning primarily because our foundation was built on resentment. My father naturally resented my mother. My stepmother's resentment for Mom bordered on contained hatred, I'm sure. And my brothers and I resented Mom for leaving us. That's a lot of resentment aimed at a person who wasn't even there.

My own feelings were conflicted. While I was upset that she gave us to Dad, I understood that she had to do it. Texas just wasn't what it was supposed to have been and as a result, she—*we*—needed help. I commended her for her strength. Unfortunately, at ten years old I saw my mom as a hero. A crusader. My own personal Joan of Arc. During those first few years of living with my father, I defended her often. But there was no room in his house for my beliefs. Pro-Mother automatically meant anti-Father, anti-home builder, anti-provider, anti-establishment. It was as if my dad had hung a standard proclamation on every wall in every room: Peppur is not allowed to perform such a disrespectful act as mention her mother, allude to the concept of her mother, or even *think* about her mother, in any context whatsoever, at any time from now until never.

I just wanted my mom back, but I didn't know how to say it. My throat hurt from habitually choking back stinging tears and trapped exclamations. I became afraid to express my feelings for fear of the explosive response I'd receive, so I kept my emotions to myself. I stopped mentioning my mother altogether and an obedient, silent, invisible me emerged. Today, I wonder how much of this metamorphosis was attributable to my stifled environment or if it was just because I was going through puberty.

Puberty or not, it was easy to be invisible. No one pays attention to a skinny, shy girl who never talks or smiles. I had sucked my thumb until I was eight . . . nine . . . ten? and was punished with buckteeth that demanded to be noticed no matter how much I tried to stretch my lips over them. Like a loud, obscene amateur comedian that just will *not* get off stage during open-mike night, there they were. From sixth grade through junior high I looked like a joke until I was rescued by years of braces and several (lost) retainers.

I BELIEVE MY STEPMOTHER NEVER WANTED CHILDREN. She is an excellent English teacher for her junior high and high school kids— always a favorite—but I think she wanted to leave all personal involvement with adolescents at school. And now there were three of them lying on her new couch, leaving socks in the living room, and breaking her dishes while trying to wash them. A mess was thrown at her and she was forced to make a home out of it. Had it been me, I think I would have left. For whatever reasons, she stayed.

We had a "mom" who didn't want to be one. We didn't call her Mom and she didn't want to be addressed as such, because as she would often say, "I am *not* your mother." I was forcibly *dis*connected from the woman who loved me as her daughter and forcibly connected to one who didn't.

To cope, my stepmom emotionally distanced herself from us in terms of motherly affirmations like affection, discipline, and companionship. In return, Dad distanced himself from her and parented double time. Or maybe Dad devoted so much energy to the three of us that he didn't leave much room for my stepmother. A huge hole was left in the center of our household, which we all tiptoed around. I felt stranded.

I needed help. Already suffering from the goody-goody good girl syndrome, I was afraid to get in trouble, so I did nothing wrong. I didn't drink until college, and I didn't have sex until after college. I didn't do drugs. Instead, I became addicted to praise. What I engaged in were activities that made people clap for me. I excelled at everything I attempted. I was elected class president twice, was prom queen, served on student council, was a member of the pompon squad, and wrote for the yearbook. I spoke at my junior high, high school, and college graduations. I was the MVP and/or captain of my college track team. I learned quickly that if I did well, people took notice. They congratulated me. They applauded. If I did nothing, I remained invisible. Which would you choose?

This tactic backfired, of course. In college, I became a star triple jumper, winning week after week for nearly seven months of track meets for four years in a row. However, the pressure of being number one finally got to me. During my senior year I went to a campus psychologist who asked, "Who would you be without track?" She wondered if the jump had gotten bigger than me. I couldn't admit the answer then but it's so obvious now. I feel like I'd be nothing without the stuff I do. I live for the challenge of setting goals and the satisfaction of achieving them. I achieve, achieve, achieve just so someone will pay attention to me.

My addiction backfired at home also. In a strange twist of events, I became a daddy's girl. We discovered that we both shared a competitive athletic drive and were both dreamers. I had also blossomed into the life of the party just like him. But this new friendship and father–daughter relationship drove a wedge between my stepmother and me, because, as I discovered later, we were competing for my father's attention. It took a very public appearance on "Oprah" in 1991 to make us face our private problem. At the advice of Oprah, the attending physician, and a studio audience, my stepmother and I were urged to spend time together—just the two of us. That idea was like wearing new nylons under scratchy crinoline to us, but it helped. We tried it and were able to become friends, and later, mother and daughter.

It was my stepmother who bought me a *What's Going On with My Body?* book, which I still have. I went to her when my period began and morphed me from girl to woman. (When my dad took me bra shopping, we came home with a nursing bra instead of a training bra.) My step-mom is also more practical than my father; she was the one that would come through for us during those moments when we needed a voice of reason. And, it was my stepmother who kept—and continues to keep—our house a home.

THOUGH I GREW TO LOVE MY STEPMOM, there were times when I desperately wanted my momma. Periodically, Mom would try to contact us and for a time she lived less than an hour away. Yet any contact with her was disruptive to the home life that had formed without her. Her phone calls were accepted with dread because now it was my father who was coaching in the background. Her letters didn't always reach our hands. And the occasional visits that were eventually allowed caused more angst than joy. And that's how it was until college when I began paying my own long-distance phone bill and receiving my own mail.

From the solitary confines of my dorm room, I could speak with her freely. We laughed, and I told her stories about boys. She told me stories too as she was now separated from my stepfather. The lines of commu-nication were open, but our mother-daughter relationship had traveled through a severe time warp. I was now eighteen and she was thirty-six. We each spent a lot of time searching for the person we had once known before we actually got to know each other again. (When my brothers reached college, they really didn't know her. They were roughly eight and six when custody changed and they had few memories of her or of us as a family unit.)

In time, Mom and I became friends again. Eventually, I thought, "My mom and dad should be friends too!" I initiated a three-way phone call between them and myself that left me staring at the phone in disbelief. My parents traded humorous, non-bloodletting insults, and actually communicated for the first time in years. A lot of tension between the two of them eased; and life became easier.

We lived and we learned. When my brother graduated college, all three of my parents were there and got along for the first time. There are still plenty of firsts to be dealt with, like weddings (assuming I ever get to and past the point where some guy actually says, "Please meet my *girl-friend*, Peppur," when he introduces me to his friends); births; and the splitting of holidays. But I'm confident that all three of my parents will no longer act like idiots. Or, maybe they will, who knows? What I do know is everyone is on their own now and I can't worry about how my entire family is going to evolve as we continue to heal from the upheaval that happened more than twenty years ago. I've got other things to worry about—*me*.

THE BLAMING GAME

Serena Kim

I AM SITTING AT A CIRCULAR TABLE in the sweltering kitchen of my Brooklyn apartment on a hot summer afternoon. Although I consider myself a diligent writer, I don't want to work on this essay right now because it is a strain to remember who was at fault in my parents' failed marriage. I've been smoking a lot of Newport cigarettes and keep forgetting to turn on the air conditioner. Although I've gone around in circles like a border collie chasing its tail, I know that I must try.

My shrink, whom I have long since stopped seeing, suggested that it was all my mother's fault—that she was a beautiful but grandiose prima donna who never dealt with her parents' divorce and her separation from her own mother. Of course my mother has tried to convince me many times that it was my father's fault—that he was a meek but selfish academic who repeatedly put his career before his family. She blames his inability to manage money and familial responsibility. She has enough evidence to prove it, too. After all, he *wasn't* there. And he never paid for child support. For decades my mother supported not just me and my two older sisters, Elaine and Mirena, but also *his* elderly mother, while he switched areas of study, universities, and ultimately entire cities. He rarely visited, but when he did, my parents would fight or he would torment my sisters with unreal expectations about where they should go to school and what they should do with their lives.

It was much easier to decide whose side to be on when I was younger. My father was the obvious perpetrator. When he was around, there was a tension that erupted all too easily. One of my earliest memories is of my parents venomously hurling insults and teacups at each other. I remember hiding under my bunk bed in our Korea town tenement apartment, and crying as porcelain shattered in the next room. Shortly after, when I was four, they officially separated, and he left for Harvard to finish his Ph.D. When I asked about his return, my mom looked at me with her lips strangely curled. "Next year," she said.

When I was five, my father was still a positive presence in my life. I longed for him to come back and teach me about Roman numerals and Greek mythology, about the animal kingdom and how to have patience. He liked to take me to colleges to look at the architecture. He told me never to let my studies slack, or else he threatened that I would end up at Cal State Fullerton or some other mediocre state school. He taught me how to waltz one night in the outdoor parking lot of a Chinese banquet hall.

In those early years, my father took several pictures of me in front of the Volvo sedan that my mother bought for him with her garment business money. I held a balloon that he had bought me at the Los Angeles Zoo on one of our happy excursions. He was proud of me.

For the next two years, I never saw him. Every New Year's Day, I would wake up hours before my sisters and jump into my mother's bed. "So Dad's coming today?" I would ask her, my face beaming. "You said, 'next year' and now it's next year."

"We'll see," she would say, still half asleep.

Thinking back on it now, it must have pained her to keep on deceiving me. I don't know what's worse—to find out that your parents don't love each other or being told fairy tales.

Then, when I was seven, my father showed up at the front door of our house. A lot had changed in those two years: my eldest sister, Elaine, had left to study at Berkeley; my mother had worked hard at her ladies' apparel store and had purchased a brand new Toyota Celica for my sister; we now lived in a fancy four-bedroom house in a tract-housing stretch of the arid Inland Empire called Walnut; I had finally put on some weight and caught tadpoles in a nearby stream; I had new friends. I had almost forgotten how much I missed him.

When he showed up one night at our doorstep like some kind of vacuum salesman, his thinning wavy hair disheveled, wearing an impossibly out-of-date striped nylon shirt, I didn't know how to react. I wasn't sure if I missed him, and I wasn't sure if I wanted him back. He was like a stranger. He told me I had to learn to cook and make good coffee if I wanted to be a good wife.

Nobody ever said stuff like that to me—things that made me feel like an object, a tool. And I felt weird wearing pretty dresses in front of him. I didn't want to please him. When I set the table for dinner, I set the worst, most chewed-up chopsticks over the yellow-orange placemats in his place. I gave my mom the best ones. When my mother went out on trips and I was left alone with him, it was I who felt homesick.

I don't even remember what they were like together. Did they sleep in the same bed? Were they affectionate with each other? I can picture my dad napping on our couch, his feet crossed, encased in thin black nylon socks. My parents were trying to get back together for my sake, but they never kissed or hugged.

About a year after he moved in, the beating happened. I must have been eight and I didn't know where he was. I walked all over the house, calling for him impatiently. And then I started to really yell for him. In our sprawling suburban home, we had a rumpus room—the kind of place where white families have pool tables or dart boards, but where we kept jars of fermenting bean paste and old mattresses we no longer used. I think my dad was trying to set up some kind of study there. He rushed out of the room, face beet red, enraged at my impatience. He grabbed me and started hitting me hard. He pelted me open-handed over and over again on my face and arms. He shook my shoulders and shouted in his scary Korean baritone. "This isn't enough. I have to get the belt." He disappeared down the hall. I heard him rummaging through his closet.

I remember running into the cool sanctuary of my mother's bedroom. I picked up the phone and dialed the number to her store. When she answered, I told her he was going to kill me. He crept up behind me and snatched the phone out of my hand. He didn't have a belt. But I ran into my bedroom, ridiculously decorated at that time in brightly colored geometric patterns. I slid down next to my twin-size bed. I cried so hard, wiping my eyes so frequently, that I got scabs on the sides of my eyes in the shape of caterpillars. Later, I learned that he used to beat my sisters black and blue regularly before I was born. My mother's hatred for my father became my own.

MY PARENTS' MARRIAGE WAS DOOMED from the jump. My young mom, a fairly successful writer of children's books in Korea, wanted out of her own broken family and the reign of her dominating father. Her own parents divorced when she was only a year old. After a series of traumatic kidnappings as a baby, my mother ended up in the custody of her father, a wealthy and successful surgeon who once threw her into the rushing rapids of a cold river to teach her how to swim. She is still afraid of water to this day. "He was only kind to me when I was sick," she has said on more than one occasion. She was not permitted to see her own mother until she was eighteen.

When she was still a teenager, my stern grandfather married a woman who was only six years older than my mother. They later had three children. Meanwhile, my real grandmother remarried and had three more kids. My mom was stuck in a sort of metafamily, in which she was born to a huge extended family but never really belonged in either part.

As soon as she got to be of marrying age, her best friend introduced her to my father, a handsome intellectual who also liked to dance a fierce tango. While I don't know exactly how they met, I do know that they were of similar quirky and cerebral persuasions. They both loved to read and debate philosophy and politics. Even though he came from a poor family (his father was a gambler and all five of his siblings had died of malnutrition or tuberculosis), they decided to get married. As a brilliant graduate student of philosophy at Seoul University, the most prestigious school in all of South Korea, he had a promising future ahead of him.

Soon after my second oldest sister was born, my father left for the States to get his master's degree from San Jose State University in California. He spent a year in Colombia while the immigration laws were being amended. My mother and sisters came out four years later. My mom, once a woman of letters, found herself making kimchee for a living in an "Oriental" grocery store in San Francisco.

By 1970 my mother was living with her two daughters and her mother-in-law in a filthy apartment above the store. Pictures of her pregnant with me in 1973 revealed her plump and greasy, her long hair parted in the center, looking like some kind of Hell's Angel smiling reluctantly into the camera as it captures the poor surroundings of our Bay Area hovel. Nubbly maroon couch. Dingy walls. She tried to stay up late to write, but she was too exhausted. My dad stayed focused in his pursuit of higher education, visiting libraries and attending conferences across the country, while also trying to conceal his discontent with her inability to be a supportive wife.

If she really wanted to write, why didn't she just write? We could have been a lot poorer and led the kind of ascetic artists' existence that I fantasize about now. But I guess we *were* really poor. And she had to negotiate between that desire for an affluent standard of living and the dim prospect of a writer's income.

While I don't remember those days in San Francisco where I was born, I do remember her as a tall, beautiful woman working in Los Angeles four years later. After her long morning shower, she would meticulously wash and condition her hair—a thick, chestnut-colored bob. And when she moved, it reminded me of a Vidal Sassoon commercial, the way it would swing and then fall back perfectly into shape. For work, she wore pantyhose and knee-length skirts with high-heeled pumps. Silk blouses with puffed sleeves and blazers with shoulder pads. I loved to watch her dress—the way she looked at herself in the mirror knowing that she was gorgeous.

But I hated seeing her put on makeup. Her features looked smaller and kinder before she piled on the thick layers of eye shadow and greasy foundation that was always a shade too light. Her eyebrows were arched abnormally high. She reminded me of some kind of femme fatale from a 1940s movie. But what I hated more than anything and what I increasingly hated more as I got older was the smug, fake smile she would give herself when finished, her hand holding the mirror high in front of her face. When I complained about the makeup, her well-worn excuse was that most of it would rub off before the day was over.

My dad was living a totally opposite life. While my mom slept on a queen-size bed in our suburban home, my father slept on a cot ensconced between Japanese linguistics books at my grandma's apartment—actually a housing project for the elderly— during his stint at Southern Illinois University. He wore secondhand clothes, and always bought me strange knick-knacks at yard sales. He listened to old Latin artists on vintage vinyl.

When they were together, they were like two ethnic groups struggling for sovereignty within one national border. They would make peace only for more fighting to inevitably break out. By the time I was thirteen, I was convinced that divorce was the only rational solution to a prolonged painful situation. I thought that once my father was completely out of our lives, my mother could be happy. I thought that I would be divorcing him, too. Most of my friend's parents were divorced, and I was savvy enough to figure out that those picture-perfect families on television were just illusions—even though they had tortured me as a kid. I encouraged her to divorce him.

But what I thought would bring relief only brought more pain and violence. My mom lost her business when the divorce papers were finally served. She felt like a failure. We moved into a cheap low-slung apartment across the street from the Santa Anita racetracks that didn't seem much better than the first ghettos we had lived in as new immigrants. Plagued by allergies and arthritis, she lay in her bed wearing a stretched-out nightgown, cursing at me for forgetting to bring her tea. She hit me pretty regularly at that time for a variety of sins—not doing the dishes, looking like my father, telling her off, hiding my report card. It further fed my rebelliousness. Pretty soon I was forging hall passes to cut class and getting Ds; I started smoking and ran with troubled white girls who had been sexually molested or abused. Meanwhile, my sisters were far away in college.

I've started talking to my dad again in the past year and a half, which is weird because since I was thirteen, I have systematically ignored him. Somehow, I figured out that hating his guts wasn't helping me any. I also realized that getting close to him doesn't happen after one breakthrough talk where we announce our long-lost love for each other and apologize for years of misunderstanding and mutual neglect. The closeness we've been developing has been awkward, little steps of brief, tense conversations where I try to be as civil as possible and ask about his new life, and he eagerly inquires about mine. Sometimes we talk about painful memories. And once he told me something about my mom that I have a hard time believing. Maybe she left it out of her memories of the past or maybe he made it up all together.

He says that after I was born, he really wanted my mom to move to Los Angeles since he was going to USC for the last leg of his graduate study in linguistics. Even though they hadn't separated yet, my mom didn't want to join him. They had a business, a 7-Eleven in the Fillmore district, the underdeveloped ghetto where we lived in San Francisco, which he says she didn't want to run anymore. She pretty much abandoned it to take up a more glamorous job as a waitress at a Japanese restaurant. She never mentioned that to me. What bothers me the most is that she always made it seem like she ceaselessly toiled away at that 7-Eleven until she raised enough money to get a house in Los Angeles where she later joined my father. She told me about the times when she was frequently held up by Jheri Curl–sporting armed robbers while tending the cash register pregnant with me. I don't know who to believe.

A few years ago, I railed on my father on one of the few occasions that he visited me in New York, just as we were trying to fashion some kind of a bond. I told him that the sense of abandonment I felt when I was a child contributed to why I was a lonely single woman who seemed to repel men. I also had a propensity for destroying any semblance of a healthy, successful life whenever it got too good. "It's your fault I'm taking Prozac," I accused him, as hurtfully and disrespectfully as I could. "I don't know how to love men since you left me. Do you think you were a good father? Is that what fathers do?" He wept.

Somehow, in the past ten years, we have all managed to calm down a lot as a clan. I've finally achieved my dream to be an editor at a magazine in New York, and imported my high school sweetheart from Los Angeles to try to forge a life with me; we've been going strong for two years. None of my family members have gotten into an all-out violent confrontation in a long time, maybe even years. We've all learned how to breathe and walk away until tempers subside. And now, I can almost say we have a happy family.

Last June, my sister Elaine held my nephew's first birthday celebration at her new penthouse apartment in Manhattan. Traditionally in Korea, the first birthday is important because so few kids actually made it through their first year of life. My sister adopted a lot of the old traditions: setting up a low table filled with symbolic fruit and rice cakes in front of an expansive screen patterned with flowers and cranes. My nephew wore a brightly colored silk costume for the occasion.

I was initially upset when Elaine told me that she had invited Dad. Mom was going to be there, and I didn't want to put her through any discomfort or stress. I also didn't want to relive the disastrous family holidays of my childhood. But when the big day came, my parents (that sounds so weird) acted surprisingly mature. They showed up alone (my mom arrived first to help prepare) and avoided each other most of the night. When they did speak, it was always with a kind of bemused curiosity. And when my boyfriend and I started to leave, they both saw us off, saying goodbye in unison. Later on, my mom giggled about how she had caught my dad trying to take a picture of her. She had felt bloated, so she kept trying to move out of the shot. "Why would he want to take a picture of me when I'm so fat?" she asked smiling, secretly flattered.

When the birthday celebration was over, my father returned to the Midwest, to his American wife and their big house in the white-collar section of Carbondale, Illinois. My mom packed up her bags and headed to her artist boyfriend's loft in downtown L.A., where they raise lovebirds and aquarium fish. It's funny, now that I think about it, how they have sort of switched their lifestyles and made peace with aspects that they used to loathe in each other.

But who's to blame? I guess at this point, it's not really about blaming. What good does that do but harden the stone of resentment that was planted in me the day I became a part of their lives—a stone that I've worked real hard to soften? It's about stomaching the chronology of events with a cold, observant eye and realizing that every human being is capable of the most mundane but simultaneously terrifying acts of ignorance. I am trying hard not to repeat the cycle. God, do not let me repeat that cycle. My sisters alternate between hating either one of my parents for their immaturity. I just try to keep from blaming myself.

THE PROTRACTED AMICABLE DIVORCE

Aaron Kunin

"YOU'RE A VERY CAPABLE PERSON," someone tells him. Capable of what? ("Very" capable—equals degrees of capacity?) Capable of anything: therefore, incapable of making a decision.

Incapable, for example, of breaking up. Incapable of wanting to break up. As though the history of his parents' marriage—their long period of separation, their unusual compromise (living on different floors of the same house) before finally divorcing (but continuing to live in the same neighborhood), then, a few years later, actually trading houses—expressed a limit in his understanding, as though this model of protracted separation was the only one he knew.

And also, without being aware of it, he does something to prevent the other person from being able to break up with him. They never fight because he never fights with anyone (incapable of fighting). Negotiating with him is an easy negotiation in that one of the parties is willing to give anything to avoid conflict; a difficult negotiation in that one of the parties would like to extend the period of negotiation indefinitely. They remain together much longer than is good for them, past the point at which they should have broken up. An unhealthy relationship. A disease that strikes relationships.

It's not because they end that they're failures. They failed while they were going on; their failure was, precisely, failure to end.

(The summary gives me so much pleasure when I write it like that, that I don't want to develop it into anything.)

Splendidly Perverse

One thing that's never easy to explain is the idea of "splendidly perverse." An organizational principle, a shared aesthetic, a *regime d'viver*, an appetite. Often it's what draws him to another person. "You seemed splendidly perverse to me!" Splendidly perverse: "That doesn't make any sense, so why don't we just do that?" Splendidly perverse: "Since we're not going to enjoy this, let's see how much we can increase our discomfort." "Let's try making this as weird as possible." This is something he learned at home. His preference for the hard uneven back of the radiator rather than a soft chair or sofa with cushions is an example.

Third Person

There's usually a third person too. He never wants more than one for himself; he's incapable of being interested, he thinks, in more than one person at a time. But the other person is often involved with still another, or becomes interested in another, and he has no objection if the other person wants to spend time pursuing the third person, since it's okay to have two if you keep both of them happy, since being interested in several people over a long period of time is not really that different from being interested in several people at once: the name for the former is serial monogamy, and the name for the latter is parallel monogamy, and both are versions of polygamy.

He doesn't understand why he and the third person should be kept apart. "I'm sorry that Aaron feels hurt," the third person says. "I still don't want to see him."

There's no precedent in his parents' marriage, as far as he knows, for the third person, unless it's the expectation that any family should include at least two households. There were, as far as he knows, no third persons in his parents' marriage for several years after it ended. Even when Michael and Linda were living in separate houses, they never got involved with anyone else. And they continued to do things together as a family: eating at restaurants or at one of their houses, going on vacations, fighting over inconsequential things, seeing the marriage counselor. If there had been anyone else, it would have been difficult to conceal him, her, them, from one another or from their children, because there was practically no place where they enjoyed privacy.

Segmented Houses

The children were allowed privacy. If one of them was in the bathroom, no one else tried to enter or yelled questions or accusations from the hallway. The children had their own rooms which no one entered without permission. (The door to Natasha's room did not close very well, but it could be propped shut.) Linda and Michael, when living together, allowed themselves almost no privacy or modesty. There was no room in the house where they did not receive their children. The room they shared was always open; it opened, in fact, into the room where the children played, read, watched TV, etc. When Michael and Linda slept, the children, who had trouble sleeping, often appeared by their bed and woke them up, as though they could absorb some of their parents's sleep for their own use; Johanna did this almost every night, getting out of bed without fully waking, appearing by her mother's side of the bed, sometimes moaning a little, apparently in distress at being neither fully asleep nor fully awake.

Sleeping Portraits

Michael and Linda sleep on their backs, sprawled across the mattress, one or both of their arms above their heads, their legs bent, twisted, the covers pushed away; Aaron pulls the covers over his head, draws his limbs together against his body, telescopes his body, so that he gives the impression of a long fold in the blanket; Natasha lies on her back, propped up at the head of the bed, sometimes over the covers, mouth gaping, arms and legs generally turned out, surrounded by pillows and worn clothes; Johanna turns on her side, forearms clasped together, her jaw working constantly.

Buyer's Remorse

The history of Michael and Linda's marriage and divorce gives the impression of increasing segmentation: first they live in the same room, then on different floors of the same house, then in different houses at a distance of one mile, then finally a few thousand miles apart. But (at least until Linda moves to a different part of the country and remarries) the individual segments have a remarkable tendency to join, communicate, and exchange members. It should be noted that there was no time in the entire history of their marriage and divorce when they were not looking at houses. That this is something they always did together as a family. That they always had at least one real estate agent. That their house— and later, their houses—were always for sale. That they also owned, together, a three-room cabin by a lake, which they sometimes visited in one another's company, sometimes separately. That they often proposed living arrangements that seemed definitive and lasting, but you learned to distrust that impression. That many living arrangements always seemed possible; and this was certainly exciting. That they might have lived in adjoining parts of a duplex. That the children might have lived in a house and the parents might have traded off weeks living in the children's house, spending the alternate weeks alone in another house. Can it be by accident that Michael will later use a term from real estate to describe the problem in his brief second marriage—"We both had 'buyer's remorse' "?

Genussmittel Portraits

Linda smokes heavily, which helps to bring on her lung condition, gives it up, and has to perform daily postural drainage exercises to get the fluid out of her lungs. She drinks coffee steadily through all her waking hours but won't drink bad coffee and gets annoyed when it's offered to her; she doesn't like to see her children drinking coffee but is slightly distressed when they don't ask for it. She usually drinks wine or beer with dinner, and will occasionally have gin-and-tonic on summer afternoons. She seems to be touched deeply by minor events (disheartened by a bad meal; even the possibility of a bad meal—a bad meal narrowly avoided).

Michael smokes heavily (cigarettes), gives it up, puts on a little weight (which is not unbecoming), switches to cigars; he also smokes pot sometimes, and does not bother to hide it from his children. He rarely drinks coffee (decaffeinated only). He almost never drinks at home, but at restaurants will often have scotch before dinner, wine or beer with dinner, or cognac after dinner, or some combination of the above. He seems to derive a special pleasure from seeing his children drink. He avoids spicy dishes that interfere with his digestion. "He has such good taste in everything except food."

Aaron drinks as many as nine cups of tea every day, and periodically gives it up for periods of a month or a few months because he doesn't want to depend on it too much, and returns to it because he doesn't want to be pedantic about it. For a long time he used to drink cups of chocolate in the morning and at night (sometimes even alternating sips of tea with sips of chocolate) but gave up the chocolate because it spoiled his appetite for food. He gives the impression, which is basically accurate, of never having touched anything stronger. It's not on principle that he refuses every offer of coffee, cigarettes, alcohol, or drugs, but because he never wants them when they're being offered to him. He likes the taste of coffee but the caffeine affects him too strongly. He doesn't like the taste of beer except as a flavoring for soup or bread, and even a few swallows sit too heavily on his stomach; he will sometimes drink part of a glass of wine or hard liquor to oblige other people. He does not smoke and has never even tried because it frightens him a little; he believes he's prone to it. He has at least one mental or physical condition for which he could receive medication but prefers to leave the condition intact. His problem, he is told, is that he doesn't believe in psychology; perhaps his problem is that he doesn't see that as a problem. He has a special fondness for spicy dishes and can handle them pretty well; also pastries.

Natasha smokes heavily and gives it up, takes it up again and gives it up again; there are worse things she could be doing. She knows how to make good coffee and drinks it sometimes but doesn't make a habit of it. She will sometimes drink excessively, but no more than she can sleep off; the effects of the alcohol may be exacerbated by the various antidepressants and anti-anxiety medications that she takes, which also cause her to put on weight, which Michael teases her about. She invariably has a bad reaction to pot and has to be taken to the hospital a couple of times, which is embarrassing, but she'll smoke up with anyone. She went out with a heroin addict for a short period but never got addicted to heroin herself.

Johanna smokes heavily and gives it up, drinks coffee regularly and gives it up and takes it up again, is prescribed antidepressants and gives them up. She often drinks wine or beer with dinner and occasionally drinks enough that she blacks out. Occasional pot use. Instructed to avoid sugar on account of hypoglycemia, she rarely follows the instructions but talks about them constantly.

Segmentation and Interlace

Example. Aaron's room is adjacent to Michael's but feels closer to Linda's, which is directly underneath. Every noise his mother produces is audible to him as though she were in the room—especially her cough (symptom of her lung condition) which invariably sounds to him like an expression of disapproval. A "nagging" cough. His noises are equally audible to her. If, in the middle of the night, he steps out of bed onto the bare floor, causing the floor to creak, his mother, a light sleeper, will awaken, cough her guilt-inducing cough, and speak to him through the one-way intercom at the foot of his bed (e.g., "Aaron. It's two in the morning. Go to bed."); the shrill dry sound of the intercom switching on, followed by her angry voice, frightens him disproportionately, no matter how much he prepares for it, no matter how much he knows that it's coming. Nonetheless, he will get out of bed at some point almost every night, because there's a book on the other side of the room that he wants to look at. (He isn't supposed to read after his bedtime but can do it without too much trouble by maintaining the fiction, which is not entirely a fiction, that he is afraid of the dark and needs to have a light on in the hall.) Before going to bed he spends a long time staring at the bookshelf, trying to anticipate what book he will want to read tonight; he takes five or six more than he could possibly want and places them carefully under his pillow, a precaution that is supposed to prevent the eventuality of crossing the room in the middle of the night, causing his mother to turn on the intercom, etc. But the book he wants at two in the morning is inevitably on the other side of the room. He will spread a blanket over the floorboards to cushion his body and muffle the creaking; he will cross the room with imperceptible slowness, shuffling rather than stepping, so that he becomes more involved in the labor of getting across the room without making a sound than in retrieving the book whose title he may have forgotten by the time he reaches his destination, but some noise will ultimately penetrate his mother's light sleep, rouse her, etc. Sometimes he will not be responsible for the noise that awakens her. And quite often, after he falls asleep, one or several of the books under his pillow will slip between the mattress and the headboard and drop to the the floor, making a terrific noise that will cause his mother to turn on the intercom, which she can do without getting out of bed ("What are you doing up there, having a party with elephants?").

Later, when Michael and Linda maintain separate residences, it becomes apparent that each house is a system that operates according to its own rules. That at Michael's house you can have a girl in your room, and at Linda's house you can't, is an example. The trouble, according to Aaron, is that the rules are not consistent; all he asks, he claims, if he has to live in two households, is that there be one code of behavior for both of them. It's possible that he isn't lying. A year later, when the practice of moving from house to house every other week becomes intolerable, he elects to reside permanently in Linda's house, where the rules are stricter, only stopping at Michael's house for dinner on nights when his sisters are staying there. He does, however, retain a key to Michael's house, and sometimes brings girls there.

A more complicated example is the back door, which can be open or shut, or, if shut, locked or unlocked. Linda believes it should be shut (bugs) and locked (criminals) at all times. Michael believes it should be open (fresh air) during the day and unlocked (for convenience: what if someone goes out and doesn't have a key?) unless everyone is away on vacation. Aaron has a key in his pocket and—his own unswerving rule of conduct—would never leave the house without checking to see that it is there; he automatically locks the door when he comes in and when he goes out, not because Linda has trained him especially well, but because something in her training appeals to a base element in his character. Natasha and Johanna are constantly losing their keys and borrowing or stealing them from one another or from someone else—not from Aaron, who never loses his keys or leaves them on the counter or in the lock (as Michael does)—and they scream bloody murder when they see that someone has inconsiderately locked the door again; they also have a weird habit of entering the house through the front door, for which no one has a key and which can be opened only from the inside: for that, someone in the house has to act as porter, which no one especially enjoys doing.

Hairstyle Portraits

Michael, who owns and manages hair salons for a living, is almost completely bald, and is deeply ashamed of this; the top of his head has, for him, the stamp of moral degeneracy that is sometimes associated with physical imperfection. He does not believe that anyone could find it attractive. His small fringe of hair is trimmed at an out-of-the-way barber shop. His neat beard, which has some copper in it, he trims himself, with an electric razor.

Linda's hair is streaked with gray starting at age thirteen; for most of her adult life it's thick, straight, and through-and-through silver, and she's been complimented on it so many times (it's the kind of effect that people call "striking") that she considers it an asset to her looks. She would never get her hair cut at one of her husband's salons; instead, she loyally patronizes a hairdresser who used to work for Michael and who left on bad terms. The hairdresser is not aware of Linda's connection to her former employer.

Aaron refuses, according to a secret principle of his own, to pay for a haircut; he will not, in fact, allow his hair to be cut or his photograph to be taken by anyone he doesn't trust completely, because in both cases the act is too intimate to be shared with a stranger. This means that the photographic record mainly shows Aaron smiling distrustfully or trying to avoid being photographed, and that only Linda and Johanna can cut his hair. He hates shaving more than anything, and if he could get away with it, would let his faint beard grow out; he would go around with a paper bag over his head if he could get away with it. Two other prohibitions govern his behavior: never to go out of the house with wet hair, and never to get into bed with hair that smells of cigarette smoke, cooking, etc. He hates the sensation of being wreathed in smoke or of being damp.

Natasha's hair is thick and dark, like her mother's before it went gray; but there's not a trace of gray in hers, which is, perhaps, both a relief and a disappointment. She often says that she wants to grow her hair out but gets impatient before it gets very long and has it cut by one of her father's employees who is also his personal friend. The hairdresser flirts with her in a way that's probably harmless; once she saw him at a party, so drunk that he was unable to pronounce her name ("Tanasha. Tanasha. Tanasha.").

Johanna's hair changes all the time; usually it's pretty short and sometimes it's colored dark red. She will let anyone cut it and sometimes does it herself; apparently she isn't too neurotic about it, which, if that's really true, makes her an exceptional case.

Central Conflict Theory

Conflict in a household is usually understood as a centralized phenomenon like the conflict between the hero and the villain in a Hollywood film. One person wants something, another person wants the same thing or another thing, and the conflict between them is a result of the obstacles they create to keep one another from achieving their goals and the efforts they make to overcome the obstacles. E.g., "You did this to me. So I'm leaving you." But conflict isn't usually experienced as progress toward a goal. I want to suggest that conflict in a household—fighting—occurs on a symbolic level. Let me be clear about this. I am not saying that each particular fight is an instance of a more basic disagreement that it symbolizes. On the contrary: a fight is a symbolic arena in which any disagreement can be substituted for any other.

Analogy. Stage one. Michael and Linda sleep in the same bed; Aaron and Natasha sleep in separate beds in another room; Johanna sleeps in a crib in a third room. Then Aaron moves into Johanna's room; Johanna takes Aaron's place in the room shared with Natasha.

Separation. Michael moves into an apartment a few blocks away. Compromise. Michael (bearing the standard of marriage and family—which I misheard as "famine") returns, sleeps in his own room on a different floor; Aaron sleeps in an adjacent room; Johanna sleeps in the room where she started; Natasha and Linda sleep where they have always slept, except that they no longer have roommates.

Divorce. Michael moves into another house, in which he sleeps in his own room, Aaron sleeps in the room immediately below, and Natasha and Johanna share the adjacent room; in the original house, sleeping arrangements remain unchanged, and Linda uses Michael's old room as a studio. Later Aaron sleeps in his mother's studio; Natasha sleeps in Aaron's old room; Johanna sleeps in Natasha's.

Compromise. Michael and Linda trade houses: Michael sleeps in Linda's old room; Linda sleeps in Michael's; the children remain as before.

They fight in the same way. What they fight about (one of the things they fight about is what room they're going to sleep in; another is piano lessons) doesn't matter. The point is that, at any moment in the fight, anyone in the family can occupy any position, in the same way that, at a given moment, any one of them may be sleeping in any room in the house or houses. This analogy is also useful because it suggests how easily a person can get drawn into a fight that seems to involve someone else. It is also useful because the fights take place in all of these rooms, and sometimes move from one room into another; there's no privacy or modesty in this arena either.

Conflicting Portraits

Michael's first response is always wrong, but he will maintain it, no matter how unreasonable it is, for as long as you oppose him. He will not listen to what you're saying, because you've become, for him, merely an embodiment of everything that you owe him (his memory for obligations goes a long way back). If you argue with him at this moment, you will not get anywhere. But if you leave the room and come back a few minutes later, you can talk to him; his memory for conflict is short.

Linda considers every conflict a betrayal. Any conflict is automatically replaced, for her, by a more basic one: "Why are you spoiling our lovely dinner (afternoon, vacation, etc.) with this fight?" When she's composed, her main task is to narrate what the other or others are doing or saying. When she's most angry, her vocabulary becomes vaguely British (once she called me a "cad," another time a "rotter"—where did she come up with these words?) She's never violent, but sometimes seems to threaten violence; if she's fighting with a child, she may chase it around the room, as though by forcing its body in a certain direction she could change the direction of the fight. She also likes to leave the room at a critical moment and have a bath or a cup of coffee while the others sort it out for themselves. Afterwards she cries.

At age eleven, Aaron resolves that he will never again be drawn into one of these pointless fights. The cost of this resolution, which in any case he is not entirely successful at keeping, is that he forgets how to fight. This means that he is excluded from the beneficial effects of fighting (such as winning, etc.) because he doesn't fight even when he should. It also means that on occasions when, contrary to his resolution, he gets drawn into a fight, he is ill-equipped to conduct himself. His deplorable habits of argument are painfully frustrating for everyone involved. He talks too quickly, but no one would be able to understand what he's saying at any speed; even he can't follow it. The fact that nothing that he says seems relevant to the fight suggests that there may be limits to the symbolic interchangeability of disagreements. Afterward, you find him leaning against the wall or pacing the floor, justifying his actions to himself.

Further results of the avoidance of conflict (for Aaron). (1) He never sees conflict or aggression. He frequently assumes that people are engaged in a balanced inquiry in pursuit of a higher truth when in fact they are maliciously fucking with one another. He is only able to recognize it after the fact; someone else has to point it out to him ("Oh, that was conflict!"). (2) And when he does see it, he likes it. He's attracted to it. He's excited by people who pick fights, get into fights, win them, etc. He only likes the ones who seem invulnerable; but if they weren't slightly vulnerable, they wouldn't be vulnerable to him; but it's the vulnerability that he doesn't like (if they were invulnerable to him, he'd like them perfectly). Such is the bitter law of his erotic career.

Whenever anyone is attacked, Natasha believes that she is being attacked. So she defends herself. Her defensiveness often prolongs fights that might otherwise have resolved themselves; it also has the unfortunate effect of drawing the brunt of Michael's anger and contempt, since Michael will automatically attack anyone who defends herself for as long as she continues to put up a defense. For this reason, Natasha maintains that her relationship with Michael is deeper and richer than, say, Aaron's, since the most Aaron will do is get out of the way.

Johanna remembers every wound that she has received, and who gave it to her. Memories of this kind are not unusual. Her special gift is to have the memory at precisely the moment when the memory of the wound will be most harmful to the person who inflicted the wound. This strategy—turning her wounds against her persecutors; using old wounds to wound others—works. Johanna also knows that the function of an apology is to reintroduce the original offense in a concentrated form. Or else the apology is directed toward the future (why else would you be so apologetic? "You're not apologizing for what you did; you're apologizing for what you're about to do!").

Graphological Portraits

Linda and Michael have almost the same writing. Isn't that interesting? Both produce recognizable versions of Palmer script, which they learned, probably, around the same time, in cities not far from one another. Linda's has degenerated, perhaps, a little further from its model; it tends to reach slightly above the upper line and slightly below the lower one. Their signatures, also, are remarkably similar in style, producing complementary impressions of speed, energy, decisiveness.

Aaron's writing is small and uneven; it draws as little attention to itself as possible and takes up surprisingly little space, like a dog guiltily wedging itself into a corner or under a piece of furniture. Over many years his writing gradually becomes more cursive but never gets larger or easier to make out. His vowels all tend to look alike, as do the letters with crossbars, except for his "*f*," which doesn't look like anything.

Natasha makes large, round letters—as large and round as she can make them; they give the impression of expanding to fill whatever space they've been put in, bulging and flapping against the margins. Her writing seems to have changed very little since she learned to write.

Johanna tends to write in small capitals. Her letters are extremely precise, regular, and efficient, without ligatures or ornaments of any kind. Neither are they mechanical: the human effort to make the letters conform is almost palpable; each letter expresses an intention. There are no secrets, shadows, or dark corners here—everything is distinct and clear—but there are depths; an impression of deep focus. Reading a document in her hand sometimes feels like being addressed by an actor—someone whose voice has been projected. Her signature is complex and probably difficult to reproduce, but it always looks exactly the same.

ROMANCE AND RESPONSIBILITY

Kelly Murphy Mason

AT AN EARLY AGE, I learned to assume responsibility for my father's romantic life. Though I'm a child of divorce a couple of times over, I've always just thought of myself as an orphan. What qualified me originally was my mother's death during my infancy. But my father's subsequent romantic disasters kept me orphaned, because in the wake of each divorce, there were hardly any responsible adults to be found. The grownups became oversized children wishing each other every imaginable ill; the youngest of us just got underfoot. My second stepmother, for instance, wished my father dead more times than I care to remember. She promised to dance on his grave. My father is dead now, so she did get her wish. I don't know whether she's actually danced on his grave. Something makes me suspect she hasn't. All those broken hearts taught me that we shouldn't trust the things we think will make us happy.

MY FATHER'S HEARTACHES WERE MY FAULT because my mother's death was my fault. Though she was killed in a car crash, childhood logic somehow convinced me that she wouldn't have died if I hadn't been born. In his briefest treatment of the subject (he never dwelled on it long, if he managed to dwell on it at all), my father explained to my older brother and me, "Your mother died trying to be a better mother to you kids." That was meant to answer any questions we might have. I was nearly twenty before I understood that he meant that she had died en route to a child psychology class at the university.

My father was well acquainted with the psychological profile of the motherless child, having been one himself. His own mother had left him and his infant brother to a man uniquely inadequate to the task of raising them. Then, in his first marriage to a bleached-blond alcoholic I remember merely as a halo of cigarette smoke, my father became the sole reliable caregiver to their children. Two survived; one was stillborn, while another was born with birth defects that would cut her life short. Destroyed, he couldn't help but blame his wife; he was already separated from Jean when he met my mother.

After he lost my mother, my father had a sizable collection of life stories he'd rather not tell; he generally told them only after he'd had too much to drink. Some of my earliest memories are of the darkened bar he and his friends frequented; at my most exhausted, I would sometimes crawl under the table and fall asleep on the floor. Later on, my father would collect me in his stout arms and carry me from the bar to the car, and from the car to the house and to bed, careful not to wake me. Sometimes I could hear him being quiet; his breathing was that shallow.

However late he stayed out, though, I think my father was exhausted almost every waking moment I knew him. Between the coffee and cigarettes and drugs and booze, he somehow got things done. But he didn't trust himself to parent my brother and me; that lay far beyond his ken. Part of what exhausted him, I'm sure, was the never-ending search for a woman who would mother us all.

ENTER THE NANNY. Her name was Joanne, and like my mother and all the women to follow, she was attractive and much younger than my father. In addition to being his employee, she was also the love interest—one of them, at least. For a while, she and her young daughter lived with us in a white colonial that I remember as gargantuan. In consequence, I recall the blaze as being far more dramatic than it probably was.

With Joanne on call, my father was gone more frequently. He was gone the night the kitchen turned warm and glowed orange and echoed with shouts. There was another woman with us, someone to grab hold of my brother; Joanne scooped up her daughter and then me. My chin bounced roughly off her shoulder as she loped down the driveway with the two of us in her arms. I'd never seen a sight as fierce as the rear of the house catching fire. Watching it, I had the sense that the end of our short driveway was receding with each stride Joanne made. Finally at the distant end, we fretted and waited, women and children, for firefighters to come save the house.

While the house could be saved, Joanne's job could not. Ever afterward, my father accused her of being dangerous. Not only did she cause the fire, he said, she once burned my brother by unwittingly putting his hands under scalding water. My brother Brian hardly survived the electrocution he suffered when he stuck his toy in his bedroom socket. Relieved of her duties, Joanne packed up herself and her daughter and drove to an apartment she had rented in a neighboring town. Since my father could not trust the hired help, he took to marrying—again.

FRAN WAS A TRAINED PROFESSIONAL, a nursery school teacher who lived two states away. Obviously impressed, my father boasted to everyone about her child-care credentials. At the time of the wedding, she was a few months pregnant; she showed ever so slightly in her empire-waist white dress. Brian was the ring bearer and I was her flower girl. Soon she would have to care for her baby son, my older brother, and me, and occasionally, the two daughters my father had had with his first wife. Barely into her twenties, Fran was often overwhelmed. I knew this because she cried easily. When she collapsed on the couch, I rubbed her shoulders as hard as I could, desperate for her to feel better.

During the night, from the top of the stairwell, I would monitor her arguments with my father. Through the rungs I strained my head for a better view. One of these nights, I started to sob. Though I couldn't hear myself through their shouts, they heard me. Seeing their faces suddenly upturned, I sprinted full-speed to my bedroom and buried myself under my pillow. Muffled as it was, the clamor they made coming upstairs was unmistakable. Then they were standing beside my bed, louder than before.

"Look what you did," my father yelled. "You made her cry."

"I did not," Fran yelled back. "You did."

"Stop it!" I yelled. "Stop it! Stop it! Stop it!"

When at last Fran took my baby brother and moved in to a local hotel, my father dressed Brian and me in our Sunday best, so we'd look almost as shiny as we had in the wedding pictures taken against a hazy photo of some faraway pastoral background. My father told us: "No fighting. Fran is very tired and we don't want to do anything to upset her. You have to be very nice to her. We want her to come back home, right?"

We did and she did, but the next time Fran left, she headed across the state line to her brother's house. Unbeknownst to Brian and me, my father had abandoned hope and found himself a new girlfriend, a gorgeous shopgirl who worked in one of the stores he owned. Fran only returned to the house to collect her things. She was not allowed to take Brian and me, though, because we belonged to our father. I was standing in the driveway after the backseat of her car had been piled full.

The oversight was glaring. "Wait, wait," I shouted. "I have something."

Running through the first floor to my baby brother's room, I climbed the bed where his Peanuts sheets lay disheveled. I stripped it with in a fury I'd not known myself capable of, and ran back outside, my arms bursting with the set. This is what I did instead of pitching myself into Fran's backseat.

"What have you got?" she asked.

"Craig's sheets," I told her. "He'll need his sheets."

"Oh, honey," she said, "he has other sheets."

"But these belong to him."

"No, you keep them," she said. "They can remind you of him."

Despite my continued stalling and her near hysteria, Fran eventually managed to drive away with Craig in tow. I was left clutching the sheets. On them was the repeating image of Snoopy asleep atop his doghouse, that inviolable home built for one.

THE GORGEOUS SHOPGIRL WAS NAMED VAHRAH MAE; before working at Papagallo's, she'd been a debutante in Florida. She had no childcare credentials to recommend her. After she'd been living with us a short while, my father told us, "Call her Mom."

"I don't want to," I complained.

"She's your mother now," my father insisted. "She's the only mother you've got."

That remained true for years. After five moves in rapid succession, it appeared as if Vahrah Mae might be a permanent addition to the household. Her relationship with my father pretty quickly soured, though, when he moved us all to Massachusetts and took a job in New York. On the Friday nights he came home, he was already scowling. My brother and I were not to bother him until after he'd had what my parents called "cocktail hour," although it was rarely that brief. My second stepmother would immediately close the door to the study and begin to flatter and entreat while she mixed him drinks. A courtesan by temperament, she intended the drinks to soothe his foul temper. Occasionally they worked. When they didn't, my father raged. "You had better shape up, all of you," he warned, "or else it's ship out."

The night Vahrah Mae started to pack for her trip to the local hotel, I sat on her bed, begging her to stay. "I have nothing to do with it," she said. "Speak to your father."

She was desperate to be gone before my father returned home; she was afraid of what he would do if he found her still home. Suddenly she stopped, hurried out of the room and then reappeared with cloth dolls we'd bought on a recent vacation to the Caribbean. The two dolls had their arms coiled around one another. "Give these to your father," she said, handing them to me, "and tell him that one of them is you and one of them is me and that we belong together, just like these dolls."

For the first time in my young life, I realized how ridiculous we all were, puppets in my father's ongoing Punch and Judy show, jittery, nervous that he'd cut the strings if we didn't perform. I had no confidence that my pleas would alter anything he did or didn't do. Long after I'd surrendered to sleep, my brother lay in wait for my father and met him at the door. "You go and get her right now," my brother told him. "You can get her back. You do what you have to do to get her back, but don't you come back without her." Oddly enough, my father took the direction. Vahrah Mae was home when we awoke in the morning.

There were variations on this scene over the next several years, each one increasingly ugly. When we all finally lived under the same roof, my father's drunken outbursts became more regular and violent, the physical and verbal abuse more dramatic. The morning I found Vahrah Mae asleep on the couch with a black eye, I discovered what my father must have known all those years: that rage has power undeniably its own.

Shaking her shoulder more roughly than I should have, I said, "Wake up. Wake up and tell me he did this to you. Because if you tell me he did it to you I'll kill him."

Vahrah Mae buried her face in her hands. "He didn't do it on purpose," she said. "We were arguing and I grabbed hold of him. He tried to shake me off and I fell back."

"If you fell back, how'd you hit your eye?"

"It's nothing," she protested. "It's not a big deal, really."

"You need to leave him," I told her. "You need to get out. I'm serious. Go."

Several more years would pass before Vahrah Mae actually did leave, years filled with crumpled hotel receipts for my father's adulterous weekends, phone calls from yet another other woman, my repeated encouragements that my stepmother leave him, her continued excuses for his miserable behavior, most especially the drinking.

My father's wineglass was enormous. More than the man at his most bullying, it presided over our dinner table. Because I could not stand to look him in the eye, I trained my eye on his glass. I watched how quickly it was emptied and filled; that told me what the night was likely to bring. But none of us knew who would get the lashing at any given meal. I was spared to a degree my brother and stepmother were not. The night my father called my stepmother a liar, I grew bold.

"Don't talk to her that way," I told him.

"Who the hell are you?" he demanded.

I'm quite sure my father didn't have an inkling. In my teens, I grew more and more to resemble my dead mother. I could have been her ghost. I think that haunted him; he avoided me where and when he could.

Yet the liquor sometimes turned him maudlin, so that he wanted nothing so much as to declare his love for the people in his life, his children in particular. One night, he was lurching through the kitchen after me, trying to capture me in an embrace. In a gesture that surprised even me, I pulled a butcher's knife from the wooden block and pointed it at him. "Don't come near me," I told him. He laughed, but it sounded forced and idiotic. "I'm not joking," I said, and he kept his distance.

My second stepmother escaped my father as I always guessed she would, at night, fearing for her life, without even a coat to keep her warm. She left the day before Thanksgiving, but she didn't leave alone. She left with my favorite uncle, my father's best friend, the man she would someday marry. Despite my uncle's declarations of love for his wife, my father blamed me for the failure of his marriage. He told me so at the last holiday meal we would share together, at the restaurant adjacent to the darkened bar of my earliest memories.

"You ruined my marriage," he said, demented with drink. "I know you think it's all my fault, but it wasn't. It's your fault. You were always a fly in your mother's ear, bzz, bzz, making her unhappy, making me out to be the bad guy, telling her to leave."

"I ruined your marriage?" I asked, incredulous. I had been away at college for three years; I was hardly ever home.

"Yes, you did," he said, nodding emphatically, righteous in the indictment.

"How did I ruin your marriage? Why would I ruin your marriage?"

"Because you hate me," he hissed. "You've always hated me."

What stole my breath? I had to remind myself to breathe; I feared I was actually suffocating. "You don't even know me," I whispered. The words required tremendous physical exertion; I felt my heart beating hard, pushing them past my lips. "You have absolutely no idea who I am. You think I hate you? I don't hate you. I've never hated you," I said. "You just always break my heart."

I pushed my chair away from the table, grabbed my coat, and left through the front door. Panicked that my father might try to follow me, I jogged for blocks and blocks through the empty streets, until I found the stray town cab that would take me back to the house, where I didn't bother to zip the suitcase I'd jammed full of every belonging I could fit inside it, and then to the bank machine for the cash I'd promised the driver for his trouble, and then to the remote train station a few towns over. I was panting the entire time; that worried the driver, who asked if I was all right. "I'm fine," I insisted. "Only tell me we can make the train. I need to catch that train." He drove like a madman, and I love him for it still. I caught the train and became the second woman to walk out on my father that holiday.

PREDICTABLY, THERE WERE WOMEN to fill the gap: the real estate agent, the interior decorator, the coat-check girl. Because I saw my father so rarely, I'm sure I missed a few. I thought it fitting, though, that they were all women whom my father met through some commercial transaction, people he paid for their trouble. Like many men on Wall Street, my father tended to regard women as commodities. Once, after I joined him and some friends for brunch, he pointed at me and asked them: "Do you think she's pretty?"

"Oh yes," they all chimed, "yes, yes, very pretty," eager to please my father by complimenting me. The interior decorator said, "Oh, she's classic, very American, very pretty."

"I never thought she was," he replied, "but you could be right."

The decorator followed me into the ladies' room. "You shouldn't take anything your father says the wrong way," she told me. "He tries. Your father is a difficult man to have a relationship with, because he's got that woman thing."

"What woman thing?" I asked.

"He hates women, you know, he's really got quite a complex around them. He needs them but he fears them and he doesn't really respect them," she said. Thinking better of it, she quickly added, "But you—he has a great deal of respect for you."

By Christmas, my father had brought another woman home, the coat-check girl he'd met at a nightclub in New York. Her name was Honor; she was younger than I and exotically beautiful. When she opened the door, I stupidly mistook her for the housekeeper. When I heard her mention my father's New York apartment, though, I realized that she was staying with him. In fact, my father had assigned her to buy me presents, thinking she'd be more attuned to my tastes than he would. Crouching under the tree, she fished for the packages she'd wrapped.

Honor was spending Christmas with us in Rhode Island because she was estranged from her family in Michigan. I had pieced that much together over the course of the afternoon. Taking my gifts from her hand, I thought my pity for her might crush me. Why would she leave her miserable family behind for mine? She was just moving from sadness to sadness.

Though I wanted to apologize for the whole mess, really, I wound up apologizing for myself. "Dad didn't tell me you were coming," I explained. "Otherwise I would have brought you something. I don't have anything for you."

"That's all right," she said. "I shopped for myself when I shopped for you. Your father is very generous, you know. You're lucky to have family like that."

She spoke entirely in earnest. The weeks she'd known my father had convinced her that she wanted to have a father exactly like mine. I never saw Honor again after that day, and my father never mentioned her to me. I didn't have the heart to ask where she'd gone.

MY FATHER CLAIMED HE'D SWORN OFF MARRIAGE altogether. When the cover story of a popular magazine gave nationwide play to a study that uncovered how many men were unfaithful, he felt somehow vindicated by it. In his finely tailored suit, sitting next to one of his corporate henchmen in some overpriced restaurant he'd selected, my father said, "Look, Kelly, it's just a fact. It's how men are. No successful man can do it; there are too many temptations out there. No rich man is faithful to his wife."

"Then I hope to marry a poor man," I said, furious in a flash. I was violating a tacit agreement between us; so long as I let boys be boys, I could be one of them myself. I no longer wanted the laurel. "Did you not notice?"

"What?"

"Did you not notice that I'm a woman?" I demanded. "Did you *ever*, in all the horrible ways you treated women, in the rotten things you did to them all, did you not ever *once* stop to think, 'Hey, I've got a daughter—I wonder what this'll do to her?' Those things you did had costs—they happened to cost me personally."

"Listen to me!" But my father already was listening; in a rare instance, he was speechless. "I'm wrecked. I'm twenty-three years old and I'm already worn out. Now you expect me to go into the world thinking every man is like you? Do you know how the world looks to me? Pretty bleak. Did you *honestly* not think about that?"

Sincerely surprised, my father tucked his chin into his collar and said vaguely, "No, I guess I didn't."

IN MY FATHER'S OBITUARY, we called her his "long-time companion." She was the last of us to see him alive. Her name was Liz; on her left ring finger, she wore the diamond wedding band he'd bought her on a cruise

to the Caribbean. She thought of herself as his wife. My father sometimes confessed that he considered marrying her. "She's a good person,"
he insisted, "a genuinely kind person." My brothers and I agreed.

But Liz was also skittish and spooked easily. I felt simultaneously sorry
for and protective of her, as I did of every woman my father brought
home to stay with him. One afternoon in spring, she called me sobbing.

"He came home so drunk, I was scared. I tried to bring him to bed
and he passed out; he just slumped down beside the bed. He's never done
that before. I thought he was dead, I really did, I kept pounding him, saying, 'George, George, wake up! George!' And he finally opened his eyes,
so I tried to help him up into the bed, but he weighed so much, it was
hard to get him up. When he got into the bed, I started to take off his
shoes, and he said, 'You know there are other women, right? You know
you're not the only one. I told you that you wouldn't be. You remember
that?' I know there are, Kelly, but he was so mean. It was cruel—he was
just being cruel to me. He'd never been like that before. I told him to stop
saying those things. Why was he so mean?"

"He's an alcoholic, Liz," I said. "He does things like that."

"I know what they think of your father," she said, suddenly angry.
"They look at him and think he's a drunk old man, a mean drunk. But I
know different." Liz told stories of how my father defended her from an
abusive ex-husband and paid for nice things for her little boys and
bought her sick sister a car and helped her plant a tree at her brother's
grave. Each story felt like a thumb pushed against some fresh bruise; I
always had to blink back my tears.

"Would he have said the things he did sober? Probably not," I
allowed. "But he's not sober. When he drinks, people get hurt—badly.
Do not get hurt, Liz. Tell him he can't treat you like that. Leave if you
have to, but you can't let him hurt you this way. No one will ever blame
you for saving yourself."

Turning positively girlish, she confided, "The other day, I was looking at your father, and he wanted to know why I was staring and I said,
'You have such beautiful blue eyes.' And do you know what he said? 'So
do you, sweetheart, so do you.'"

ONE GRAY MORNING, I stood in the cemetery where my mother was buried and waited for the gravediggers to inter the cremated remains of my father. The rest of the family had dispersed after the committal service the parish priest had grudgingly performed, but I couldn't stand to leave the miniature mahogany box alone. It made my father seem so inconsequential. When my uncle had declared that my father had wanted his ashes scattered in the ocean, I had—intending no irony—responded, "Over my dead body." My father would have a resting place, a safe and solid patch of earth. My sole solace was the idea that my father was finally out of pain. I wouldn't have to worry for him anymore. I only wanted to know where to find him.

Inexplicably, my ex-boyfriend had insisted on attending my father's wake, funeral, and committal. He was standing at my shoulder, bundled in his dark suit and overcoat. I had forgotten he came along. I was surprised when he spoke. He said, "You don't need to stay."

After a couple of years, he knew me well enough to recognize that my modus operandi had generally been to bolt. I preferred flight to fight. I bolted from our romance as I had bolted from nearly each one before and after. I wanted to get out, I suppose, while the structure still stood, before it collapsed and buried me alive. No matter how good and kind the men I dated were (and they were, each of them, in their own measure), the house was still burning down. In my imagination, the women and children hadn't gotten to safety. My heart would never stop sounding its alarm.

"I am not leaving him there. They need to put him in the ground," I insisted. "What are they doing over there? When does their coffee break end?"

"I think they're waiting for us to leave."

"If they'd only break ground . . ." I said. "So he's not forgotten altogether. I'm sure this isn't what's supposed to happen."

In the ground, my father would be reunited with my mother. My childhood was not marked by fantasies of reconciliation; truth be told, I had nary a one. But at twenty-eight, bereft, I found the notion of my mother and father being together, inseparable forever, nothing short of thrilling.

A couple of years earlier, to celebrate my completing a graduate program, my father and Liz and my older brother and his wife had traveled to my college town in the Midwest. The restaurant I picked for dinner was cramped. It was the season for getting degrees, and congratulatory crowds were everywhere. Through this throng, a fragile but dignified elderly man steered his wife with his hand on her elbow. Though it hardly seemed possible, she was more fragile than he. They were somebody's grandparents, I guess; they made me want to weep.

"I see them," my father told me, speaking softly. "I see couples like them on the sidewalk, or out somewhere, they're holding hands. They've been together their whole lives, practically. They've grown old together and one won't outlast the other by long, because how would they survive? They breathe for each other. I see them and I think, 'I would have liked to have had that.' And I would have, too."

"If your mother had survived, I would be with her today," he promised. "We would still be together. I know that. But that wasn't in store, I guess. Other things happened." He shrugged, as if to say, "I have no quarrels with life," though he did, of course, even to the end of it. "We can't pick what we'd like."

At the time, no condolence seemed deep or wide enough. None seems deep or wide enough today. Sometimes I wonder how any of us dares to love anyone at all. My father was foolhardy in a way that I cannot be, knowing what I know, having been tutored by his marriages. My early life taught me that the risks of loving all too often outstrip its rewards. As I grow older, I hope to someday forget that lesson. What could be more romantic?

The Way We Live Now

STORIES OF THE WHEEL

John Stinson

FOR A LONG TIME, MARRIAGE AND DIVORCE didn't matter to me. They were like the economy or relations with China—inevitable topics of discussion that impacted us all to one degree or another but remained distant from what I considered my actual life. Divorce was the bigger topic, but it was all the same to me. People married. They divorced. My parents divorced—no big deal. My policy toward it all was laissez-faire, Vonnegut's distant and ironic "so it goes." The whole thing was a wheel game, fifty-fifty, and people knew what they were getting into from the start. I thought this until I decided I might want to play sometime. Then the game began to look dangerous and unfair.

Part One: Devil May Care

Jimmy A.'s parents were divorced and he lived with his mom. She was too busy working at fitting into her jeans and applying Retin-A to supervise our afternoon activities, so we spent a lot of time playing Neil Young songs while we smoked pot and drank Colt 45. We didn't talk much about his dad or the divorce. Neither seemed as big a deal as our good-looking diving coach or the Dead shows Jimmy was making plans to see.

Andy C. also lived with his mom and we partied over there a lot. Andy's mom was omnipresent but hands-off. She looked out for us, but she wasn't very stern and probably believed that boys will be boys. We talked about that divorce between ourselves and with her. The consensus was that Andy's dad just had to be with younger women, so good riddance. That made a lot of sense. Apparently his dad has the same problem today and it's causing him a lot of headaches.

David M.'s parents divorced and I didn't find out until a couple of years later. I had kind of abandoned David socially to go look for girls and he never brought it up. It wasn't a surprise when I found out—David's dad never seemed to be around much when we were tight—but I was surprised he hadn't mentioned it earlier. I figured it was no big deal. Nowadays I don't think that's true.

The parents we talked about most were the ones who didn't get divorced when we thought they should and the parents who kept getting divorced. These offered a lot of debate and stories to tell. My sister's best friend, Molly W., had a dad who was a confirmed philanderer. They were very wealthy, so her mother was sure to come out smelling like roses. We were talking about this fifteen years ago, but they are still married today—to everyone's amazement and continued discussion. My best friend in college, Peter H., has a set of parents who just can't stop fighting. Wonderful people, they are both the epitome of stubbornness and arrogance. Regular discussion topic, still married. My friend Maggie T.'s mother is a divorcer on the level of Liz Taylor. With her you can keep a play-by-play—from falling desperately in love all the way through settlement. The same goes for Tim B.'s mom, but I haven't seen him since eighth grade.

When I was in high school, I think I liked divorced households. Somehow the authority seemed suspended, whether the kids lived with Mom or Dad. Things were less official and the family identity was dissipated. I dated a girl named Mira K. and even though her mom was mean and tough, it was always a lighter task to call over there and invite her out for a night of shenanigans. Compare that to Betsey N.'s family where I would go over and have dinner with everyone. My responsibilities were a whole lot clearer. She had a lording father, but it was more the complete picture that made drinking and fooling around suddenly register as bad behavior in my heart.

We talked about divorce a lot. Whether someone's parents would get divorced; that someone's parents should get divorced; how someone's parents were together in the first place regardless of their status now. We sometimes spoke on the topic in hushed tones because we had all been told that divorce has a significant impact on the kids, but I remember that the topic was commonplace. It was often painful and weird for my friends and peers whose parents were in the middle of it, but a divorce was never like a death, which always seemed unusual, sudden, and tragic.

It may be that divorce struck me as commonplace and not a big deal because my parents were not yet in the throes of it. When they did split, though, I thought of it as totally appropriate and long overdue. While everybody else's parents were divorcing or getting settled into the lives that came after, my parents didn't appear very happy with one another, and I naturally speculated about whether they would rise to the occasion and end it. I remember having very rational discussions about it with my sisters. We all just thought they should. The household wasn't in turmoil. There were problems, some significant, but things were relatively stable. My parents just didn't get along so well anymore and they didn't appear to have much love left for each other.

I was in college when my parents finally separated. I was on my own and the division of the house had very little immediate impact on me. Family dinners, arguments, cutting up, television watching were no longer part of my daily life. This furthered my relaxed attitude on the matter, and I didn't worry too much about my siblings. My younger sister was the only one left in the house and she was off to college the following year. All four kids were launched and off to the next phase of their lives, so why not my parents, too? The timing was perfect. It would make for a very tidy and low-impact divorce, civil and appropriate.

I was really coming into my own in college and my take on marriage and divorce became completely businesslike. The two were linked variables in the equation of life. If you chose to marry, you risked divorce. Divorce was not a bad thing or a setback, no more so than marriage. Both were neutral in and of themselves, just possible factors in the unfolding lives of Americans. Any judgment depended on the individual case. Someone might get into a bad marriage, then the divorce would be good. Someone might get into a loving marriage but something terrible would intervene (alcoholism or a dead child), then the divorce that followed would be bad. Bad marriage with no divorce is bad, good marriage with no divorce is good. There were millions of combinations with all the factors of life, and that is what marriage became, a chance operation in a larger equation, an operation inextricably linked (if not always leading to) divorce. The pair were parts of a wheel game. Sometimes you got red, sometimes black. Why should I take it any more seriously than that? I was in my twenties and I was testing what I knew. I had no thought of marriage myself, so the whole thing became a set of circumstances, another sociological lens through which to view the world.

There was a brief time when my parents' divorce overwhelmed me personally, but even that was oblique. The summer after I graduated college, I lived with my father in a rented townhouse. The divorce had just completed all its legal hurdles, my parents had sold the house I grew up in, and my father had moved into this place with twenty years of the family's stuff. There was a hell of a lot of it and it covered every inch of floor space not reserved for transit or loafing. There was furniture, sporting goods, toys, albums, photos, stereos, mattresses, Christmas decorations, knickknacks and heirlooms, financial records, coin and stamp collections, toiletries, art projects, dozens of jackets and coats, tools, telephones, and anything else you can think of. It was all inert and gathering dust. It depressed the hell out of me and I wanted my father to sell it all to an estate agent, get rid of everything and start fresh.

At the time, I was also dating a girl from college. She wanted to get married. She knew that already. I was nowhere close to that. I hadn't done anything with my life. I wasn't sure I ever wanted to put that variable into the equation of my life, but I knew for certain that I didn't want to then. I juggled the relationship for a few more months, then I did with her what my father never did with any of that family stuff: got rid of her and moved on.

At this point, divorce as a subject became even more commonplace. I was out in the world, dating and moving from job to job. Over a few years, I met a lot of folks and heard about a lot of divorces. I think most people in their mid-twenties can present the outlines of their parents' divorce without feeling like they've given up too much personal information. It's first-date fare: what neighborhood you live in, what your job is about and how your boss measures up, where you grew up and whether your parents are still married, triumphs and fiascos experienced over recent vacation trips. In fact, I was more comfortable talking about my parents' divorce than I was admitting where I went to high school. That information might say something about me that I didn't want the new person to think.

If I grew closer to people, my coworkers or new friends or girlfriends, I would tell them some of the uglier details about my parents' split. We would speculate about the effects of my situation or their situation. I would talk about that summer at my father's with all the stuff and say that is probably why I refuse to live with more personal things than I can pack into a midsize sedan. Still, I was cavalier. I mostly talked in terms of my equations and theories. And why not? It's easy to be cavalier when you have no intention of committing to anything.

Part Two: Devil's on My Trail

I changed and that's my trouble. I matured, grew up or something. Altered my perspective, lost my hubris. Now I think I want to get married and my theories and equations just don't look cute anymore. The trouble is I can't dismiss them, especially since I came to want to commit by going through my own precursor to divorce. I am reluctant to tell it, more reluctant than I can say without turning nasty. I hate the irony that spending half my life talking about divorce like it was the evening news has ended in my not wanting to say a word on the topic at all. I don't want to—not about me or anyone else. My story isn't special and I won't plead that it is. I went through a heartbreaker, something fourfold more common than divorce, but it had its significant effect.

Hope was the woman I was dating that summer after college, the girl I got rid of. I didn't do a very good job because less than two years later, we were back in touch and then dating long-distance. I lived in New York and she was back home in Cleveland. In short order, I was packing all my stuff into the car (it still fit in a single load) and moving to Ohio in spite of the protests of my New York friends. They couldn't understand why I would leave the big city and they didn't believe anyone could be happy in Cleveland, Ohio, no matter how in love he might be.

I went anyway. I had broken up with Hope once and I needed to show her that I was committed this time. She needed that and it seemed appropriate to me. I didn't want to go to Cleveland, but moving was a sign to her—and to me—that something had changed. I am not sure now that it had.

Something must have changed, though. Why did I want to show I was committed? I knew Hope was on the marriage track, and I went to be with her. Why would I do that unless I was changing in my views and desires? What did I expect to do in Cleveland beyond building a life with her and focusing on my writing?

Within four months, Hope and I bought a little house. I didn't want to get engaged yet, but I went through with buying property jointly. Somehow it struck me as an acceptable half-measure. It was a fixer-upper in a transitional neighborhood. We became urban pioneers (much to the terror of her parents), a young and strong couple bringing renewal (and higher property values) in the form of drywall, paint, and hardwood flooring. This gave us an identity, a project, and some momentum, all of which further convinced me that I had made the right choice.

Still we never got engaged. I knew she wanted to. I knew her parents wanted us to (her mother so she could plan a wedding, her father so his daughter would cease living in sin). Cleveland in general struck me as a "get-married, keep-house" kind of town. Still, I couldn't bring myself to do it.

I lived with Hope for two years when I decided it was time. We had a house and two cats. We were working hard at trying to understand each other. I was almost twenty-nine and it just seemed like the right course. I could not say how I arrived at this place, but there I was and marriage was the next step.

It took me two more months to ask, in mid-October. When I did, she was happy and we had the package. We had decided to sell our fixer-upper because it was wearing me out. We contracted to buy a brand-new place two blocks away (to the further dismay of her parents) and began choosing stoves and floor tiles and paint. We planned our wedding. I was at ease. It all seemed nice.

We didn't make it past spring. She discovered an employment opportunity out West. It was her dream job and she was determined to pursue it. I didn't like the idea. It was too much, too fast, and I was more interested in the two of us stabilizing. I could not stand the idea of transitioning again at her insistence, just when I was building a life in Cleveland, and she was adamant that she could not miss this opportunity. In the aftermath, people have said to me that one or the both of us set things up to fail, that we created a situation and took positions that ensured the demise of our relationship. Regardless of such theories and any talk of who was wrong or who was right, Hope and I split after a protracted breakup and made our ways to opposite ends of the country.

We had a little divorce. I don't intend to mock the real thing by saying this. There were property and assets, legal obligations, contracts to resolve regarding our wedding, two cats, and our dog. We both had significant hopes and expectations. We didn't have decades together and I had never fully made a commitment to her, but the split was long and complex and painful.

I moved back to my hometown of Baltimore. I moved into my father's semipermanent home, a different townhouse from before, an organized one purged by my sisters and brother of some of the detritus of the past. I was there alone, since my father spends summers in the Northeast. I felt good. I had no obligations, I was home to write, and the world was full of choices. I could date or not, sleep around or not, commit or not. I was nearly thirty, and I was better-looking than I ever had been in my life. I knew because I started looking regularly. This time, everything really was right.

I dated a little. I fooled around with an old friend. I quickly discovered that I was different. Hope had changed me, or being with her and going through it all awoke something I didn't know I had. I knew clearly that I wanted to commit to someone, to the right person, and maybe even get married. Understand, I was not pining for Hope. I felt secure in that outcome. I knew I could not be happy with her in the long run, but now I wanted to find someone with whom I could be.

Many aspects of the topic of divorce still anger me. The idea that marriage and divorce are "learning experiences" on the long road to self-discovery dismays and enrages me, especially nowadays. A mocking corollary to this is the "starter marriage," the hilarious notion that young folks often take up a doomed commitment that will lead them to a better one once all the smoke clears. In golf parlance, it's called a mulligan, the more focused do-over tee shot following the horribly botched first attempt, for which the golfer is not charged. Despite loathing these things, it occurs to me that I learned a lot from my near-enough starter marriage. I learned what I want and how I want it.

I did not start wife hunting. I didn't feel desperate or mercenary. My approach to everything was just different. I looked for different things in women and quickly grew more decisive. I wasn't in a rush, but I also felt for the first time that I didn't have time to waste. I also thought about a whole host of new questions. That was when I concluded that I am vastly knowledgeable about how and why to get out of a commitment, but that I know very little about how and why to stay in one.

Now I hate the topic of divorce. It is so easy to speak about and yet it is painfully personal. I have not given much detail on my parents' split because I can't report it fairly. I often think it didn't affect me much, at least not as much as some other family issues, and still I could write a five hundred–page book chronicling it all, a book I am convinced would teach nothing to anyone—not even me. I can talk for hours and hours about people splitting up and the reasons and the results. Like most folks, I am extremely familiar with it.

Staying married is a tougher topic, one I can only keep alive for a few sentences. My mother's parents were married nearly seventy years. My Nampaw's death was the only thing that stopped them. They stayed in love for most all of that time. It is a superhuman accomplishment, and I have no doubt their souls will rejoin when Namaw goes to her final reward. My friend Mary S.'s parents have been married for more than thirty years. For a while there, it looked like they might split, but they weathered it. With all the kids out of the house, they seem to have a renewed love. Mary thinks it's cute and a little goofy. How did it all come to this? It's a mystery to everyone.

I have been doing research because this suddenly matters to me. I ask married friends, my peers or mentors, how they stay married. I always get a thoughtful pause. I always hear the statement, "It's a lot of work." Sometimes I am told that luck or faith or even inertia play a notable role. Everything is shrouded in mystery or half-understanding, and the answers are always brief. The best thing I have heard was from my laconic Swiss friend who said, "I stay married because I love my wife and I choose to stay with her." Sounds great, but it doesn't edify me to the degree that the hour-long story of his first marriage's demise does. I surely know why that relationship didn't last.

I don't think there should be a school for this, and I don't believe that life would improve if marriage were an irrevocable institution. Still, I am nervous, and I'm generally not a nervous person. I think that one day soon, I would like to be married, but the numbers on it aren't good and the anecdotal evidence is far worse. I can muster some faith and my constitution is suited to all kinds of work, but I have no substantial instructions on how to employ them. I could, I suppose, buy a book, but like most people, I learn better by example and by practice. What book would I trust anyway? I know I am going to meet someone I like and that my hard-won knowledge will tell me she's the kind of person I want and get along with. Then the knowledge gathering will begin again as the two of us learn how to stay together, forewarned but not very forearmed. That's what my mentors and elders would tell me: The path is made by walking.

Recently, a friend told me that I am more screwed up than most children of divorce because my parents split so late. This was a new idea to me. My conception was that younger kids take a worse beating because of their tender age. She argued that children are more resilient and that they learn better and faster how to cope with the new circumstances. She also said that late divorces usually mean longer years of uncertainty and instability. She said that all her friends who had late-divorced parents seem more scarred than those who were children of early divorce. That got me thinking, but not so much about how "scarred" I am. Really, it just sent me back to the idea that although we talk about divorce constantly, we learn very little about how to make a viable commitment.

A note on my parents: neither remarried. It's been ten years since they separated, and neither has so much as gone on a date or made any overtures toward another partnership. My parents are both vigorous people, if not exactly outgoing, and both are very interesting. They have approached no one and they each have turned down suitors. To a large degree, this is because they have something to protect, a mode of life, their specific ways of doing things. I suspect they each harbor some WASPish sense of dignity that says it's unseemly to date at their age. More than that, though, I am certain they don't like the odds and the potential trouble they spell. My parents both learned that they couldn't bear to go through it again. It is a silent lesson to me (neither has told me why they stay single), but a powerful one. It may be the most powerful and definitive aspect of their divorce to me.

I will get married, though. If I meet the right person and we get along, I will go ahead into this commitment. I know this and I am glad of it. Still, I don't want this to be a gamble, black or red, fifty-fifty. I want to know the rules so I can play better, so I can win or at least survive. I want to dismiss the notion that it's a game altogether now that I am a potential participant. That is the cry of a solipsist. I am certainly guilty of that. It's a lack of faith and of courage, two things I probably will need to make a marriage work.

I'm getting there. I am just sobered by all the talk and very aware that the chances are that I will simply become another story, the long kind— interesting, but not good.

CHOICES

Ayana Byrd

I DON'T RECALL ACTUAL INCIDENTS. Instead, my memories are of trash bags of clothes by the front door, missing toiletries in the bathroom closet, extra space in the coat closet. Probably because it was too painful for her to face, my mother would let days pass before mentioning the obvious—that my father had once again moved out while I was sleeping, at school, or roller-skating around the block. And then, inevitably, there'd be the talk, the question put before me as if I actually had a vote in what would happen next. "Do you want Daddy to come back and live with us?"

For sixteen years, thirteen of which were during my life, my parents went through a nonstop back-and-forth, together-not-together, I-love-you-I-love-you-not that still amazes me any two people could find the patience to maintain. My mother, Stephanie, was best friends with my father's youngest sister, so she knew my dad, Sam, from afar, pretty much her entire life. Being seven years older, my father hardly noticed the pudgy ten-year-old with glasses who used to play on his porch. But at twenty-four he returned from the Air Force, married his high school girlfriend, had a daughter with her, got a divorce, and noticed a beautiful seventeen-year-old he'd somehow managed to overlook all those years.

It was impossible for my mother to expect her family to excitedly welcome her new boyfriend. A family from the same Philadelphia neighborhood, they were more than aware that Linda had a brother Sam—a handsome, divorced artist with a child. So my mother told them that she was dating someone named Frank Williams and, since they didn't know what Sam looked like, went so far as to bring him to the house, introducing him as Frank. Only her older brother knew, and he used the information to bribe and blackmail her. Finally she couldn't take it, eventually deciding to face the consequences of coming clean. But by then my grandparents had decided that my dad was a decent person and my parents had fallen in love.

Anyone who has read even one book on psychology could have predicted my mother's attraction to my father. She was born to a mother who had married Al, a handsome loner who became increasingly emotionally detached when he felt like it. Her mother had married and had eleven children with a handsome emotionally detached loner named Bruce. Sam was just the latest handsome loner for the Epps women.

I don't know enough about my father's life to draw pseudo-Freudian analyses, but in my mother he got a woman who was more than determined to establish a "normal" home and life. So they moved in together, and started creating a home that in snapshots plays back like a 1970s period film—Afro'd black people living among mud clothed pillows, wicker home furnishings, and massive record collections. But by nineteen, my mom was pregnant with me and for reasons no one has ever explained to me, she moved back to her parents' house to prepare for motherhood.

There are many who believe that our parents are no accident, that we don't just wind up with two people because of a fateful meeting of egg and sperm. Instead it's said that before conception we, our spirits that are hovering somewhere, choose the two people to whom we are born. The reason for selecting them over the countless other pairings is that through and alongside this set of parents we are meant to learn and experience certain lessons during this life incarnation.

Maybe for some that concept seems sadistic, when you look at some of the people that have children. But for me, it's a relief and comfort. It forces me to stop feeling like a wounded child and instead try to detach myself and figure out what it is that I could be learning. Instead of seeing my life as something that has been decided upon before me, it becomes a challenge or test that I get to face.

I don't know if it was my father's aversion to marriage or my mother's sneaking suspicion that they weren't necessarily a good idea, but the two never walked down the aisle together. They were legally wed by common law and we were a family unit as much as anyone else I saw. My parents are neither perfect nor evil. They always said that they loved me, congratulated me on looking pretty *and* being smart, kissed and hugged me often. Weekends at the park, chaperoned class trips, and school plays were normal occurrences, yet we always fell short of *Cosby Show* bliss.

Though they never argued in public, there were generally problems and tensions under the surface. My father tended to be in a good mood only when he had money, but as a painter starting his career there was no guaranteed paycheck. Meanwhile my mother had always envisioned her adult life as a housewife in a nice house and a husband who took care of the money. Instead, she was the main provider, on the wages of a secretary.

But money wasn't the major obstacle that they had to overcome. There were always other women, calling the house or being spotted in public with my dad. Growing up, I had no idea, even though I eventually discovered that the women I'd always known as Dad's friends, women that I spent time with, had been dating him. By the time my brother Taj was born, when I was seven, Sam was secretly seeing the woman who would eventually become my stepmother.

Secrecy was the constant theme. Secrets about the women, about my father's comings and goings, and as I discovered when I was ten, there were even secret sisters. Most kids find out about siblings with a "Mommy and Daddy are having a baby" talk. I found out that I had another sister when she was already sixteen years old. One night I was sitting on the couch with my parents, watching *Mork & Mindy* when her name came up because she was considering a summer visit. "Who's LaTonya?" I asked. "Your sister in England," my mom said, not even taking her eyes off the television. Apparently each thought the other had told me about my father's oldest child, the result of a fling he had when he was single and living abroad in England. No one caught, or at least chose to acknowledge, the look of shock and hurt that must have crossed my face and the night went on as if nothing had happened. I spent the next day crying to my fifth-grade teacher Miss Greenberg about how crazy it was that no one had told me I had a sister. When I finally met LaTonya, I experienced the added shock that she was half-white, a glaring omission considering that I had never even seen my father talking to a white woman, let alone dating one. It makes sense that my one-time Black Panther–follower mother wasn't rushing to announce her man's white child.

If LaTonya had been the only absent sister, then my parents would still be together. But sometime around their sixteenth anniversary, my mother learned from friends that my father had two small girls by two women, only six months apart. After years of always looking the other way or believing him that "this time it would be different," I think the embarrassment and rage that overtook my mom led her to the breaking point. Oblivious to what was happening, I went to New York to spend a summer with my godmother, and when I came home my father was gone.

I'm sure that I did not believe it was final. Without even consciously thinking it, I just assumed he'd eventually move back in. After thirteen years, it was a part of how things were. I didn't even ask what had happened, preferring to go on as if everything was fine. But weeks and then months passed, and my only contact with my dad was when he would call to say hello to my brother or me. At some point I asked my mother for his phone number, but she would never let me have it. She couldn't bring herself to tell me that he was living with one of the mothers of his youngest daughters. Never the most consistent man, my father would sometimes call five times in a week and then disappear for a month.

Full disclosure did not come with the breakup. Just as there was not the sit-down about my older sister in England, no one told me about the two youngest or my father's live-in relationship. It wasn't until almost two years after they split that the truth started to be leaked to my brother and me. I was leaving to spend a year as an exchange student in Belgium and my father was taking me out for a goodbye lunch. He pulled up in his car with a cute four-year-old asleep in the back. "Who's the little girl?" I asked. "Your sister Talauren." She thought I was great and wanted to spend the entire meal sitting on my lap and playing in my hair. I was shocked and could barely chew my food because I was literally choking back tears.

"What would you think about your dad getting married?" he asked at the end of our day together, as I was getting out of the car. Umm, what could I say? It was a throwback to my mom's attempts to make me feel included in the decisions to let him back in the house. Maybe another type of kid would have answered insolently with "I'll hate you forever," daring him to now maneuver around my veto of "our" decision. But, still reeling from the discovery of another sister, I mumbled something noncommittal. Months later, in a letter that my mother sent to me in Europe, I discovered that he'd actually already been married when he put the question to me. From the wedding album that my stepmother enthusiastically showed me during the first months of our meeting—when she desperately tried to bond with me—I learned that the ceremony wasn't any rushed City Hall affair as I'd imagined, but a big backyard affair that must have taken months of planning and included Talauren as the flower girl. I handed the album back to her after looking at only two pages and said I really wasn't interested, a sentiment I carried with me for years.

AS A LITTLE GIRL I LOVED the Hayley Mills movie *The Parent Trap*, where Mills played twin sisters, separated in infancy when each parent takes one after getting divorced. The film centers around the twins' efforts to reunite their mom and dad. I was not one of the many children of divorcees who lay awake in bed scheming about ways to reassemble the family unit. Instead, after years of shakeups and reconciliations, I was more interested in making sure that my position with both parents was secure. With my mother, it was no problem—her love and commitment to her children were solid and unwavering. But my father often seemed to be slipping away, and I desperately wanted for him to need me in his life as much as I needed him in mine. Just as my mother had been determined to dig in her heels and do what was necessary to be the woman that he stayed the most committed to and the one he truly loved, I had to be the one of his six children that he stuck with. In an ideal world there would have been enough love and attention for all of us, but I had spent a lifetime watching how my father operated and knew that his focus was limited and his attention span alarmingly short.

The tragedy of my parents' relationship isn't that it ended, but that I have held onto my pain and taken as normal the more destructive behaviors in which they both engaged. Today, happily in a healthy marriage, my mom prides herself on having broken the pattern of loving the wrong man that seems to curse the women of my family. Unfortunately, it wasn't until she had already taught me through example that loving someone who reciprocates only when the mood strikes is sufficient and that there is always room for forgiveness, no matter what the wrong.

In my own love life I've followed the cliché of the girl who grew up without a father in such obvious ways that my lack of originality is almost embarrassing. The Psych 101 patterns have led me to men who are needy but cover it with a veil of emotional detachment. So I give (and give and give some more), figuring that I'll fix everything so perfectly that they'll want to and have to stay.

There was Kamal, my first love, the tortured poet, a long-distance boyfriend who needed to know my every move in order to feel secure but was always managing to disappear or forget to call. As I became increasingly independent in my new life at college, he threw an ill-timed tantrum in the middle of finals to protest my not being around. When I didn't respond properly to the accusations that I was distant, he pulled his trump card and dumped me. Two days later Kamal called back, read me a beautiful poem he'd written about our kindred spirits and said he wanted me back. But forty-eight hours of not being asked once where I was going or who I was with had alerted me to the existence of an easier life, and I told him things were better this way.

Next was Miguel, the rebound guy. He was the exact opposite of every man I'd ever liked before or since. Miguel was Mr. Martyr, believing that love was a sacrifice, and maybe—only if you were lucky—was happiness a result. After five months I grew bored and distracted, moving on to Jon the gigolo. The first time my mother met him she said Jon was no good and that he reminded her too much of my father. She couldn't have been more right. Jon was beautiful, sexy, and confident, and he seemed "deep," a necessary ingredient for my twenty-year-old libido. He turned out to be a shallow player with a sense of humor that hadn't progressed past fart jokes. The one amazing thing about Jon was the astonishing number of women he managed to sleep with during the relatively short time we dated. For one year I stayed with him, forcing myself to believe half-truths and outright lies, always giving him the benefit of the doubt in seriously shady situations. I had become a bad blues song.

Valentine's Day marked the beginning of the end for Jon and me. I was at school in New York and he was living in Philly. All day on campus I watched happy couples, hand-in-hand, on their way to dinners, carrying bouquets, teddy bears, and chocolate. I, who had a boyfriend, celebrated February 14th by handing in a paper on the economic pros and cons of legalizing prostitution, mopping the kitchen floor, and watching the silent phone. Not a rose nor a card crossed my path. And the phone didn't ring once. At 8:00 I turned off the ringer and went to bed, my final thought being, "I don't need this shit."

One week later I sat in a Philadelphia restaurant eating falafel with Jon, the ominous specter of Valentine's Day looming over us. As he talked on and on about something trite and obvious, I suddenly felt my chest tighten. "I can't breathe," I gasped, initially thinking I had heartburn. But no, it was Jon. "You make it so that I can't breathe. [gasp] I am having a physical reaction to you. [wheeze] I have to leave." Ignoring that he was looking at me like I was insane, I walked out and spent my last $10 on cab fare home.

Only in movies is such a dramatic exit the real finale. But things were never the same after The Falafel Incident. I became increasingly aware of the blatant similarities between Jon and my father's philandering, and their seeming inability to stop. Every day I would try to figure out what I was doing in this relationship. I wasn't in love with Jon and the sex was at best average. The problem was my bruised ego. I refused to be just one more woman in his life. I wanted to be the one he never forgot, the one who truly mattered. It had become a challenge, another thing to try to control by accommodating myself to whatever situation arose. As I'd witnessed my parents struggling for years, I wanted to think that I could dictate the outcome through sheer effort. Fortunately, I finally broke it off and moved on, scared that I was capable of putting up with so much unhappiness but proud that I could also walk away.

During the year I had subjected myself to Jon, my mother had started dating Stan, the man who would become my stepfather. Nights that I would spend at a club, eyeing how close Jon was dancing with one woman or clocking the length of his conversation with another, my mother was learning that love could happen without drama, deceit, or suspicion. In the seven years since she'd split with my dad she had figured out that her life wasn't a 1950s sitcom. She had discovered that she could do it on her own, had been for the past twenty years, and that if she stuck to her terms a decent man just might appear.

I watched her go on a date with one of the city's most prominent businessmen who had been after her for years but thought that she'd be satisfied with a slice of pizza and a fountain soda. Years later, during his failed bid for mayor, I giggled and called him *Domino's* every time I passed a campaign poster. There was also the two-year renewed relationship with her high school sweetheart who wined and dined her, taking her on incredible, romantic trips but thinking that a family-size microwave was the perfect Christmas present for a woman with a strict "no appliance" gift-giving rule. He got dumped after refusing to stop occasional dalliances with his ex-wife. Although my brother and I silently thanked him each time we microwaved a bag of popcorn, we were both glad to see him go.

But Stan was different. He wasn't the slick, smooth playboy who usually turned up on the doorstep. Instead, he was honest and hardworking. His big flaws were that he talked way too loudly and wore

mega amounts of cologne (both of which my mother has since miracu-
lously halted). Once I remembered that the windows had to stay down
when I sat next to him in the car to avoid getting nauseous, I hoped that
Stan was going to stay around.

At twenty-two I stood next to my mother as the maid of honor at her
wedding to Stan. His son from a previous marriage was in the role of
best man. Tears streamed down my face from the moment I began the
walk down the aisle and did not stop until it was over. Some people probably thought I was mourning over my parents, grieving the fact that they
could never be together again. In truth, I was so overwhelmed with joy
for my mother that all I could do was cry. This was what she'd always
wanted. A church wedding, a simple man with no hidden kids or agen-
das, someone to share the pleasures and challenges of life. In sixteen
years with my father she had never had any of those things for more than
a few moments, and so I cried for my mother's fulfilled wish. Of course
in every wedding photo I appear blurry-eyed and puffy faced, probably
looking like I hated Stan and had been forced to attend at all.

But today, on the surface, things are very different. Our once insular
family unit of four has expanded to include stepparents, half-siblings,
stepkids, and extended family. Holiday dinners, birthdays, and graduations have us all together around the table. Outsiders are amazed at how
well everyone can get along, but it's not so hard to understand. I believe
that when my mother saw that my father acted in the same ways with a
new woman, she stopped blaming herself for his behavior. She forgave
herself and moved on. My stepmother shed any jealousies she harbored
once it dawned on her how completely my mother does not want my
dad. My father is just happy that no one is looking at him suspiciously
and Stan is secure enough to know that what's past is past.

That leaves me, still grappling with some of the unanswered questions of my adolescence and unresolved resentments about how certain
things were acted out. But it also makes me a woman who can remember that, for the most part, her parents always tried their best. If it's true
that we all chose these parents for a reason, then my choice was to learn
that even when love isn't perfect, it's still love.

RECENTLY, ON A VISIT TO MY FATHER'S sister's house, I spent the evening looking through photo albums documenting his entire life. Examining pictures of him as a child, I couldn't help but wonder what his relationship with his own parents was like. Seeing him holding me as a baby, I imagined him forming ideas about the type of father he would be. It was with a bittersweet urgency that I realized how much I needed my father in my own ongoing story, as he and his conflicted behaviors are as much a part of me as anything that I could create.

LOOKING BACK, MOVING ON

Amy Conway

EVERYTHING CHANGED IN AN AFTERNOON. When I was thirteen, my parents gathered my brother and me into the kitchen after school to tell us that our father would be moving out. I'd had no idea that their marriage wouldn't last forever—but then again, neither had my mother until a few weeks earlier, when she discovered my father whispering to his girlfriend on the phone in the middle of the night.

Twenty years, three stepparents, and countless crying jags later, the story has no ending. I adapted, just as they say kids do. But divorce is more than a crisis to be worked through. No matter how well I weathered the storm when it was at its worst, I still emerged dripping with its effects, and feel a bit waterlogged to this day. Old doubts and questions linger, and mingle with fresh ones that arise as my parents and I get on with our lives. Married myself and seven months pregnant as I write this, I now fervently hope that my husband and I can give our children a life so solid they won't even think to question its foundation, like the one I knew until that afternoon.

MY OLDER BROTHER, ANDREW, AND I were raised in a suburb of St. Louis where the leafy streets, old brick houses, and diverse, liberal community attracted academic families like ours. We played hide-and-seek after dinner with the neighborhood kids while the moms chatted on the front porches. We piled into the car for long trips to Maine or Florida in the summer. We read lots of books, watched too much television, and got "Excellents" on our report cards. It was a model 1970s middle-class upbringing, an utterly carefree existence. Only occasionally did we get glimpses of how lucky we were, when we saw that our Christmas tree had a few more presents beneath it, that some fathers bellowed at their children, that a few of our friends wore keys around their necks to let themselves in after school. But mostly, we took our happiness for granted, because we were fortunate enough to be unaware that anything else was a possibility.

Andrew and I weren't the only ones who assumed that our life would go on that way. When my parents separated, other families were shocked, and questioned their own stability; kids said to their parents, "If Amy and Andrew's mom and dad are getting divorced, are you going to, too?" There hadn't been a moment of tension or discord in our house. My parents never fought. Later, I realized that I also never saw them hug or kiss or hold hands.

I WOULD LEARN THAT WHILE MY PARENTS worked well together as mom and dad, they weren't so good at being husband and wife. They had been high school sweethearts and continued dating while my father went to Princeton to study philosophy. After graduation in 1960, they got married, for less than romantic reasons: after so many years together, it just seemed like the next step, especially since it meant my father could pursue his Ph.D. without accepting more money from his own father. So, like many women of her generation, my mother worked, as a secretary, to support them while he continued his education and pursued his career.

They were just two young people doing what they thought they should be doing with their lives, not analyzing every move and mood as today's hyperaware twenty-somethings do. But it soon became clear that their divergent personalities—she is outgoing, social, and emotional, while he is quiet, wry, and intellectual—did not make for a perfect fit. He wasn't satisfied, and she felt inadequate, burdened with the responsibility to become the wife he wanted, someone more bookish and academic. Many years later, he told her that if he could have snapped his fingers to undo their marriage in those early days, he would have. Of course, it would have taken more than a magic spell or a wish, but he could have left then, before they had children, with much less trouble and heartache than at any other moment later in their relationship. He decided to stick it out, even after having a brief affair. My mother came back to him after he wrote to her proposing a fresh start. He quoted John F. Kennedy: "Let us begin."

Andrew was born in 1965, I came along a few years later, and soon afterward we moved to St. Louis, where my father got a job at one of the universities. As a parent to young children, my mother had found something to quell her insecurities, something she was wonderful at and loved to do. She mothered us passionately. Having read an influential 1960s book that extolled the virtues of never saying "no" to children—the idea being that kids would understand their every need and desire is valued— she was permissive and encouraging, and generally delighted in the sweet, gentle boy Andrew turned out to be and the more independent child I was.

My father went along for the ride. He was active in our lives, if in a passive sort of way. He planned our family vacations, drove me to the drugstore several times a week to check for new Richie Rich comics, and helped us with our homework. But mostly, he was just *there*, bent over the kitchen counter sipping grapefruit juice and reading the newspaper in the morning, sitting at his desk sipping vodka and writing or grading papers in the evening. He was a constant, reassuring presence. He has always been a night owl, and I would fall asleep feeling safe because I knew he was still awake, somehow protecting us.

The fact that they had little in common aside from their love for us was disguised for years by the rhythm of everyday family life. Our house was a cheerful place, with the doors always open for neighbors to come on in, a cat and dog underfoot, and all four of us home for dinner. It didn't seem odd that my parents didn't spend much time together alone, rarely went out to eat or to the movies. My mother's friends were the women down the street, my father's were the professors in his department, and with their extended families across the country, there were few people they socialized with together. I can recall having a babysitter only about three or four times in my life—our parents were simply always home. They nurtured us, not their relationship.

This version of family suited my mother just fine. My father, however, still wanted more. He found it in a colleague, a cerebral woman several years younger, never married and without children. I don't know whether or not he planned to leave my mother for her, whether or not he would ever have summoned the nerve. I expect my mother did him a favor by discovering their affair. She did his dirty work for him.

He seized the opportunity, though, telling my mother that he hadn't been happy in years, that he wanted a separation. After a few weeks of tears and trips to a marriage counselor, my mother gradually began to realize that he meant it. Even so, she hoped she was just calling his bluff when she told him that it was time to speak to Andrew and me; she thought the prospect of facing us would make him change his mind. It didn't. So there we were, perched on bar stools in the kitchen as my mother said that they had something to tell us, something very sad. I could see how nervous she was, which scared me. But she managed not to cry as she said that my father would be moving out. My dad's voice broke as he quietly backed her up, assuring us that they both loved us as much as ever. Andrew acted nonplussed, and would soon head off to a friend's house. I burst into inappropriate laughter, out of fear or panic. I vaguely recall thinking that such a crisis—worthy of a Judy Blume novel!—was sure to make me the center of attention among my eighth-grade friends.

DURING THOSE FIRST FEW MONTHS my mother was out of her mind. She gathered together all the letters my father had ever written her and dumped them in a heap behind his new apartment. If both his and his girlfriend's phones were busy, she would have operators make emergency interrupts, over and over and over again. But of all the emotions she felt, she was not depressed. She realized that she had been depressed for years, and now that feeling was replaced by sheer terror. My father had taken care of the house and all the bills—she didn't even know who held their mortgage. She was also struggling financially. My dad paid child support and helped with other expenses, but there just wasn't much money to go around, with their salaries (she had started working full-time as a secretary several years earlier) now paying for two households. She took a second job as a salesperson in the hosiery department of a local department store a few nights a week. She hated it, and came home worn out from dealing with the customers like the woman who tried to return pantyhose stained with menstrual blood, claiming they'd never been worn. My mom didn't argue with her. She just wanted to make some money and get back to Andrew and me.

She did her best not to show us how out of control she felt. And in general, our parents tried to do everything right. They assured Andrew and me that the separation had nothing to do with us, didn't badmouth each other, and had me see a child psychologist. Talking to someone impartial helped me identify my fears and feelings, and I enjoyed the notoriety of being picked up after school to go to the shrink. (My brother, just starting his senior year of high school, refused to see the psychologist, and in general played the part of aloof teenager.) My father moved into a small apartment across town—the girlfriend was on sabbatical in another state, so we didn't have her to worry about right away—and we set up a visitation schedule. Andrew and I would see our dad on Tuesday and Thursday nights. Andrew often skipped it in favor of band practice, but my dad would pick me up, take me to Steak & Shake or to his apartment where we would make dinner. I would do some homework, we would watch TV, and he'd drop me off back at home a few hours later.

It was just assumed that we would live, seven nights a week, with our mom, in our house. Perhaps my father didn't want to disrupt her life any more than he already had, or maybe one or both of them realized that he wouldn't know what to do with us on his own (in fact, my mother recalls that Tuesdays and Thursdays were chosen in part because they were "good TV nights"). But the arrangement took away the thing my father was best at: just being there. With no overnight visits, there wasn't a room for me at his apartment. Gone were the familiarity, the routine, the security. Instead we had dates, with chats about things that didn't help us get to know each other better, but just showed how much was missing.

It was a strange transitional year, as we picked our way through the remains of our broken family. The following fall, Andrew went away to college, I began high school, my mother adjusted to being a single mom, and my dad started living with his girlfriend. We were moving on, each of us on our own.

HAPPILY MARRIED PARENTS often don't seem like real people to their children—they're a mom-and-dad unit, balancing each other's strengths and weaknesses to present a single parental personality. Divorced parents are all too real. They're actual individuals, full of foibles with no one to compensate for them. When my brother went away to school, I was left alone with these two new people. I got to know too much about her and not enough about him.

If she were a religious woman, my mother says now, she would have prayed for me when I was a teenager. Without faith to fall back on, she hoped that trusting me would be enough to see me safely through my high school years. She didn't feel like a match for a strong-willed daughter, and after our permissive upbringing, she couldn't exactly become a disciplinarian. So she offered what she always had: love, support, and too much freedom.

In truth, my adolescent antics weren't any more scandalous than those of my friends, but because in my house, rules and discipline were replaced with openness and communication, I didn't have to sneak around as much. My mother, for example, started dating someone seriously around the same time that I did, when I was a junior in high school.

When she would spend the night at her boyfriend's house, she suggested that mine stay over with me so I wouldn't be alone (she had already used her mom-radar to pinpoint almost to the day when I would lose my virginity, and had taken me to the doctor for birth control pills). She was often too candid with me, telling me more than I needed to know about her life and trying to be too hip about mine, and I strained for the kind of privacy afforded by more conventional parents who pretend their teenagers aren't turning into adults.

One of the reasons my mother was so lenient with me, she says now, is that she felt a nagging fear that I would go and live with my father. She needn't have worried. It never would have occurred to me. On Tuesday and Thursday nights, I was now going to the house that my father's girlfriend (who would become his wife after a few years) bought, where the two spare bedrooms were their studies—again, there was no place for kids. She was smart and interesting, but not warm or gregarious, like our mother. She had no idea how to react to her new teenage stepchildren and settled on being aloof and somewhat cranky. The first time I went there on my own, I knocked on the door, feeling awkward. Neither of them said "Don't be silly! You don't have to knock!" Forever after, I would knock, always aware that I was only a visitor in this house.

My father certainly didn't treat me this way intentionally. Without my mother's lead to follow, he didn't seem to know what to do—and he didn't have it in him to be the leader himself, facilitating a relationship between his children and his girlfriend. He was kind and gentle, as he had always been, but seems to have given up his role as an authority figure in our lives. He didn't offer guidance or opinions, never told us what to do or made a rule. Andrew and I craved more involvement and attention from him. Though we knew that our father loved us, we didn't understand why he didn't seem to care all that much.

If my relationship with my mother was volatile, noisy, and emotional, my relationship with my father was unfailingly polite. Of course, this drove my mom crazy. While she agonized about how to raise me and had to put up with my adolescent tantrums, he only had to worry about what to serve me for dinner twice a week. She also had to console me when I came home from his house and burst into tears because he was so detached and uninvolved. It still drives her crazy, because in many ways, Andrew and I are stuck in those roles that we assumed fifteen years ago. She is still the one to listen when we're frustrated and insecure, wondering why he rarely calls, has come to New York one time in the eight years I've lived here, and, most of all, why he doesn't seem to take his rightful joy in having two successful, happy adult children, not to mention a grandchild on the way.

We rarely ask him these questions. We have tried on occasion, like the time when I was in college and planned an elaborate speech telling him I wanted his input on my life, wanted a closer relationship. I cried through every word of it, only to have him and his wife respond defensively, essentially denying any truth to my feelings. During a less explosive conversation, he said that he just didn't want to interfere, that he himself had an overbearing, bullying father, and knew that we were getting plenty of parental feedback from our often overly involved mother. So now, instead of trying to change him, we try to remember that this is just the way he is. It doesn't make it any easier.

THOUGH OUR RELATIONSHIPS WITH OUR PARENTS haven't changed drastically since we were adolescents, much else has. Our mother has remarried and divorced, and is more content today, single, than she was with either husband. Our father is still searching. He left his second wife for a third several years ago, and divorced again recently. The experiences of watching my mother and father go through the messy machinations of dating, attending their weddings, and being saddled with stepparents and stepsiblings have ranged from mildly unpleasant to traumatic, though I don't think such events have to be upsetting. If either of my parents had made solid matches, exploring new relationships could have been wonderful.

In my own romantic life, I've had one serious, long-term boyfriend after the other since that first love in high school, but I wasn't always faithful. Whether this was because of what I saw in my own family growing up or simply youthful indiscretion, I don't know. Meeting the right person could be what broke the pattern. When I was in my mid-twenties and had recently moved to New York, I met the man who would become my husband, a remarkably solid and secure person (with married parents), and was soon thinking about the future. Marriage didn't scare me, perhaps because I remember my own early childhood as being so happy. And I can see how different my marriage is from my parents'; it's a true honest partnership. But there are still echoes from the divorce. The idea of my father telling my mother, too late, that he had been miserable for years haunts me. I have rather irrationally made my husband promise to alert me immediately if he feels an inkling of dissatisfaction with me—if I'm not smart enough, too smart, too fat, too thin, too short, too tall—so I have the chance to change.

My husband and I already feel like a family, just the two of us. When our child arrives, we both want to provide the same thing for this vulnerable little person: a loving, stable place that insulates against the rest of the world. The only difference is that in matters of family, my husband has the confidence, or perhaps naivete, that comes from being brought up in a home without divorce—the belief that once married, you stay married. I know better. I just have hope.

ROOTLESS

Michelle Patient

I MET MY HUSBAND WHEN I WAS TWENTY-TWO, while I was in graduate school in England. I was having a pint of lager with a friend in an on-campus bar when I spotted this guy dancing across the room to a James Brown tune he'd just put on the jukebox. He was funky in a hippie sort of way, with waist-length, dark-brown hair, and sad gray eyes framed by long, ostrich-like lashes. He was exactly the type of guy that would raise my Republican-voting military family's eyebrows. Perfect.

I nudged my friend and pointed him out. She said she knew the guy that was sitting with my longhaired crush and would be happy to do some investigating. The four of us then quickly spiraled into an awkward middle-school-love drama, just short of passing notes that say, "Do you think so-and-so is cute? Check yes or no."

My crush and I ended up having a couple of pints together the next evening, with a large group of our friends watching from a short distance, lined up like a jury. Sam was a second-year undergrad studying math because, he laughed nervously, he was dyslexic, and his mother was Jewish so he'd been "clipped." I was sold—after all, what else do you really need to know about a guy besides whether or not he has a learning disability and is circumcised?

We ended up talking till about four in the morning at an impromptu party in a friend's dorm room. I let Sam crash in my room, because he was too messed up to drive back to his shared house in town. We kissed the next morning, and started dating, if that's what you want to call lying in bed and drinking gallons of hot tea with milk and smoking spliffs and sleeping together.

It lasted a few months, and then Sam suddenly broke it off with me one night in a pub because he said he was scared to sink deeper into a relationship that would have inevitably required long-distance pining away or a dramatic goodbye. He said he wanted to stay friends, but I didn't believe him, because everybody knows that's a classic bullshit line.

But then he put his money where his mouth was by pursuing a platonic friendship with me. He'd invite me over to his house to watch TV and play board games, or stop by my room, and almost nothing changed except for the lack of physical contact. I was frustrated, but I took what I could get.

I flew to New Jersey at the end of the school year to finish my dissertation at Rutgers, my alma mater, as I'd run out of money. Sam took a job with an Anglo-American work exchange as a camp counselor in the Poconos. He visited me a few times, and after he left my apartment for the airport to fly back to London, I shocked myself by spontaneously bursting into tears. I then swore my baffled, staring roommate to secrecy, as I had just gotten back together with my pre–graduate school boyfriend and I didn't want him to find out.

Early the following year, I scraped some money together and bought a plane ticket to England to visit Sam and some other friends. Being back was such a high, and I wanted to move back. And unresolved sexual tension between Sam and me was creeping out of the woodwork. I didn't have a British work permit, and I knew there were only two ways to solve that problem, since I wasn't a political refugee: have a specialized work skill that no British person had (like being a Swiss watchmaker or being Madonna) or get married. And since Rolex wasn't beating my door down and I can't sing, and Sam liked the idea of being able to work in

America, he and I figured a green card wedding would solve the problem. That sort of arrangement didn't bother me one bit.

MY PARENTS WERE BOTH TWENTY-TWO when they got married. On paper, it was a sensible match: they met at a party at Fort Meade, Maryland, where their fathers, career Army colonels and decorated World War II and Korean War veterans, were both stationed. They were a promising couple, the handsome, clean-cut, red-blooded young American lieutenant and his beautiful blonde nurse wife, bound for a respectable life of duty, honor, country, and the perpetuation of family tradition. Trouble was, my mom hated the idea of being a military wife: teas, fundraisers, socializing, all in the name of boosting your husband's career. Life under a microscope. She was depressed for most of their seven-year marriage. My dad, now a retired lieutenant colonel and an obstetrics and gynecology hospital administrator, with hindsight, thinks she had postpartum depression, but it's too late now to know for sure.

My parents got divorced in 1975, when I was five. My mom was regularly seeing a Me Generation therapist who told her that getting a divorce would be the best thing for her. I don't remember whether my parents told me they were getting a divorce, nor do I remember the day my dad moved out; I only remember him no longer being in our suburban townhouse in northern Virginia. My mom got custody, and they divided up their cars and furniture and record albums in a relatively civil manner, and both got on with the business of looking for new spouses. Mom would later say that Dad got off easy because she naively asked for a child support amount that didn't increase with inflation, so it eventually ended up as peanuts.

Dad would pick up my two-year-old brother Joe and me on weekends, and we'd stay at his new apartment, which he shared with a divorced high school friend. I thought his high-rise apartment was glamorous, but the only memory I have of my father and me together in that place is of him yelling at me to stop jumping on his bed. (He didn't understand that it wasn't just random jumping, but rather a one-woman performance of the entire Snow White story, thank you very much.)

My dad introduced us to his girlfriend Joyce, a tiny blonde secretary and occasional Barbizon model seven years his junior, for the first time at her apartment, and she was nervous. She buttered up to us by giving us giant store-bought gingerbread men. Fortunately for her, we were an easy sell. The four of us got McDonald's and went to the park. She ran around the playground with us, and sang songs, and was very chirpy in a Snow White sort of way, and I liked her.

I was oblivious at the time as to what the consequences of her relationship with my dad might be—I just thought she was another week-end person who could take us to Farrell's for ice cream. My father recently tried to rationalize his and my mother's divorce as a positive thing, because it resulted in "just more adults to love you." Dad likes happy endings, all neatly packaged and tied with pretty ribbon. It wasn't his idea to get divorced. So I suspect that it's just too painful for him to even consider the possibility that the split had anything other than a happy ending.

When my father and Joyce got engaged in 1977, she was terrified to tell her father. Connie was a slow-speaking retired blue-collar worker whose days consisted of gardening, leaving brown lumps of wet chewing tobacco in random places, and watching the TV shows he circled first thing in the morning in *TV Guide*. Joyce grew up in a tiny mountain town outside Altoona, Pennsylvania, the youngest of six in a working-class Catholic family. It was the kind of gothic old-school Catholicism that consisted of bloody, sad-looking martyrs, rosary chanting, and Virgin Mary lawn shrines. Marrying a divorced man with a seven-year-old and a four-year-old just didn't fit into that picture.

To Joyce's surprise (and this is a story my dad loves to tell and retell in his Hallmark card fashion), her father's first question was, "What about the kids?" I don't know what old Connie meant by that, but my father thinks that we were his primary concern. I really don't have any reason to doubt that, because he always made us feel welcome in his house, and he once told Joe that he loved him, which was unusual for a rough-around-the-edges guy like Connie.

As the wedding plans proceeded, my brother and I hovered politely in the background—waiting, waiting, waiting—while Joyce and my dad looked at reception halls, tasted cakes, picked flowers. We weren't included in the ceremony. We didn't sit at the front of the church; we sat halfway back, in the middle of the crowd, with aunts and uncles and close friends.

My dad and new stepmother, who had already been living together, moved into another high-rise with a mutual friend. Gloria, their roommate, had dark hair, and all three were incredibly corny and earnest, so their living arrangement resembled *Three's Company*. I loved to visit my dad, because, as was the case with so many noncustodial parents who get weekend rights, we got to do fun stuff like go out to eat or sleep on the floor in sleeping bags if we felt like it. There was no schoolwork or chores, and Joyce was good at entertaining little kids. And after a year of weekend visits in the high-rise, the Army sent my dad and his new wife to Germany for a three-year tour.

MY MOM GOT REMARRIED IN 1978, in a small ceremony at a friend's house, to a Navy officer she met in a bar. We sat next to them at the wedding. He moved into the townhouse my mom and dad had bought together, but then we moved to a rental house in a neighborhood across town shortly afterward. Don was from Georgia, and we didn't really know him because we hadn't been included in the courtship. He had very red hair—or so we thought. One afternoon, our neighbors invited our newly blended family, which included our new stepbrother Chris (who was a year older than me and came to live with us from Guam, where his Navy stepdad was stationed), over to their backyard pool for a swim.

Don took a flying jump into the deep end, and shot to the bottom, but his toupee chose to stay on the surface. The neighbors tried to be diplomatic by pretending they didn't see what looked like a drowned baby fox, but Chris, a precocious blond tornado of a kid who was forever in trouble, yelled, "Look at Dad's hair! It's floating!" and screamed with laughter. My brother and I were confused, but we laughed too, because Chris was our idol and we followed his lead. The silver lining to Don's cloud was that he no longer had to disguise his baldness in the privacy of our home. He would rest his toupee on its stand on the back of the toilet, and walk comfortably around in his boxer shorts and v-neck T-shirt, his Velcro toupee attachments still glued to his bald scalp.

Joe and I loved having Chris around, because he knew the funniest insults and thought of the best games to play, whether we were in the backyard or the backseat of the car. He was always roughhousing and laughing and racing around. I was jealous of Joe because he got to share a room with Chris; I thought they were always up to fun stuff after we were all sent to bed.

Chris once told Joe and me about a game he learned from his younger stepsister Britt called snuggling. He said that in order to play, you just took off your clothes and lay on top of each other. It sounded kind of boring to me, but my mom caught Chris suggesting to Joe that they play this game one evening while they were in the bathtub. She was very upset, and Chris got a harsh spanking.

The traits that my brother and I found so attractive in my stepbrother were exasperating to my mom and stepfather. Chris was forever being punished—the preferred method in our house was to write things like "I will not be late for dinner" fifty times in a row. He was the star of sitting at the dining room table, pencil and notebook paper in hand, but I guest-starred on a fairly regular basis. We would cheat by writing one word at a time in a column, thinking that this made the mind-numbing repetition pass quicker, but if we were caught, Mom and Don made us begin all over again.

The ultimate threat of punishment was a belt whipping, which was introduced courtesy of Don's southern background. I was absolutely terrified of being hit with his thick, wide 1970s belt. Joe and I never "got the belt," but Chris did a few times, and I was scared to death for him when I heard his howls and the slap of leather against his bottom coming from the master bedroom.

Chris's mother and stepfather returned from Guam, and he was sent back to live with them. Joe and I never saw him again. Meanwhile, Don had left the Navy, and accepted an engineering job near Tampa. So in the middle of my third-grade year Mom and Don traveled south to look for houses, and Joe and I went to stay with my father's parents in Maryland for a month. My mother sobbed uncontrollably when my grandparents came to pick us up; I cried quietly with my face buried into the fabric of their Oldsmobile's backseat, as I didn't want to upset my grandparents or my brother.

MY FIRST DAY OF ELEMENTARY SCHOOL in Clearwater, Florida, was awful. I felt like I was stuck in one of those weird dreams where you have no pants on, and can't get home no matter how hard you try. We had moved into a four-bedroom ranch house in a neighborhood behind a car dealership, after living for a few months in an efficiency motel near Don's job. It was good to be out of the motel, as I'd had to share a bed with my brother, and he always kicked in his sleep.

Don's parents lived four hours north in Jacksonville, Florida. Because Don was in the Navy reserves, we'd go up there one weekend a month so he could work, and we'd stay with Herb and Mary. Herb was a cigar-smoking man of few words, and he had the same hair pattern as Don. Originally from Indiana, he was a manager at the Winn Dixie grocery store around the corner.

Mary came from a big, poor Georgia family, and she spoke in a slow, shaky Southern drawl. Her head was always cocked to the side due to neck pain, and she spent her days smoking long Carlton cigarettes and polishing her fingernails in front of the television. She always went to the bathroom in the dark with the door open, and she wore a brown bouffant wig. She also made a mean Sunday dinner, and it was there that I developed a weakness for heavy Southern food like ham, sweet potatoes, and corn bread. (Years later, after we lost contact with them, Mary was found drowned, floating face down in their screened-in swimming pool. Don's family thought it was an accident.)

Staying with Herb and Mary was boring, and it seemed as though my mother was always either sleeping or out doing something without us. We'd watch hour after hour of TV—this was where I first discovered MTV, and I was obsessed—and I'd apply and reapply Mary's nail polish to my fingernails and toenails. Sometimes Chris's cousin Travis, who was two years younger than I, would come over. He was sort of a brute, but Joe and I figured it was better than having no one to play with, so we put up with the arm burns and the head butts.

Back in Clearwater, my brother and I slowly made friends, as kids who move into new areas usually do. My mom got a nursing job working nights in an emergency room. She'd just be waking up as we came home from school.

Don left for work before we left for school. He didn't like to be bothered. He'd get up before anybody else, and read the paper (which I was forbidden to touch until after he was finished—I was a voracious reader) and drink coffee. After work, if he wasn't playing racquetball with work friends that we never met, he'd watch TV in his trademark boxer shorts and V-neck T-shirt. (He'd stopped wearing his toupee in Virginia, and just went with his natural bald look.) We started to address him as Dad, at his insistence. I didn't want to, but I didn't want to get in trouble for arguing.

At dinnertime, Mom and "Dad" would eat watching TV in the living room, and Joe and I would sit at the kitchen counter. I always read books during dinner, as I wasn't that interested in making conversation with my little brother, but I'd hide my book under the counter because Don would always make me put it away.

My mom was disaffected with her second marriage. She told me, years later, that she'd known immediately after the wedding that her marriage to Don was a mistake. She had been terrified of being alone, and thought that no one would want to be with a woman with two kids, so she settled for the first man who came along who wanted her.

One time when I was eleven she and I were lying on her bed, and she tearfully asked me what I thought she should do about Don. I listed some pros and cons and consoled her, telling her things would be fine. I was secretly wishing like crazy that she'd leave him, because I perceived him as an intruder who slept with my mother and didn't give a crap about how Joe and I felt about things. Don wasn't cruel or abusive—he just didn't care. I eventually got my wish.

DURING MY EIGHTH-GRADE YEAR, I went to Maryland, to live with my father and Joyce, who had returned from Germany the year before. We saw them three times during their time abroad: Joe and I flew to Europe one summer to see them, and they flew home twice to Maryland, to my grandparents'. I wanted to spend more concentrated time with my father after his long absence. Joe stayed in Florida.

My mother was terrified that I would never come back, so she made me sign a contract promising that I would only stay with him for a year. I was only too happy to sign, as I didn't want to repeat a scene we'd shared in Virginia when I was seven. She had come into my room to kiss me goodnight, and I told her that I wanted to try living with my dad for a while. She burst into tears, grabbed me by the shoulders and shook me, shrieked that I wasn't allowed to leave, and ran out of the room. I was bawling, as I thought I had done something really bad, and then Don came into my room with tissues, and told me it wasn't my fault, that Mom had just had a bad day. It was the only time that I can remember him showing genuine heartfelt compassion.

I had made a few friends in Maryland while visiting my dad the previous summer, but for all intents and purposes, I was the new kid again. Apart from the usual middle school cruelty and bitchiness, I adjusted fairly quickly, because it had been my decision to move.

My dad and stepmother had had a son the summer before, so I shared the house with my one-year-old half-brother, Brett. I spent my spare time hanging out at the mall with my friends, wearing too much black eyeliner and Jordache jeans that were three sizes too small, and smoking Marlboro Lights in the woods. Brett toddled around the house, watching "Winnie the Pooh" four times a day, and drinking gallons of apple juice. When my dad had told me Joyce was pregnant, I was indifferent, but I came to like my half-brother, as he was a funny, good-tempered little kid. I also started to call Joyce "Mom." It just seemed like the appropriate thing to do as time passed, and I thought her feelings might get hurt if I didn't.

I came home from visiting a friend's house one day and my father and Joyce asked me to sit down. They told me that my mother had called, and she and Don were getting a divorce. I was happy that he would be gone when I moved back, but I knew that it would be weird if I responded gleefully, so I did my best to act "maturely concerned." After I allowed them to finish their consolation speech, I called my mom, because my real concern was whether she was upset, and she was okay, almost relieved. She told me that she had given Don my bed, an antique double wooden frame that had belonged to my great-grandmother. I felt cheated, as nobody had asked me whether I wanted him to have it. When my mother and stepfather got to the obligatory possession-divvying stage of their divorce, I certainly hadn't expected my own personal things to be thrown in as well.

I only saw Don one more time, when he took Joe and me out for an awkward postmortem dinner, and then he moved to Arizona.

I MOVED BACK TO FLORIDA, and except for the three of us having to live on my mom's modest nurse's salary, Don-free life was great. I started high school, and had very little supervision and a 12:30 curfew. My mom was busy dating a guy named Steve, who was the father of a girl on my soccer team, so she was happy to let me get on with my own life. I'd cheerfully announce Friday evening that I'd be gone until Sunday afternoon, and my mom would cheerfully kiss me goodbye and go back to wining and dining with Steve.

My best friend Kelly lived in her childhood house with her nineteen-year-old sister, who would buy us a couple of cases of Busch and go out for the evening. Kelly's mom had moved to Ohio to be with her boyfriend, and her dad lived in Texas. So we would spend every weekend inviting friends over, smoking loads of cigarettes, and playing quarters until someone threw up or passed out, and then starting all over again the next night. The freedom was exhilarating. It was like having Peanuts parents: absent adults with droning voices who never interfered.

But then my mom decided to get hitched again.

Just after the school year ended, Mom and Steve got married at a Methodist church. Both our family and Steve's family were Catholic, but the Catholic Church wouldn't perform the marriage without annulments, and as Steve had also been married twice before, that would have been a hell of a lot of paperwork for both of them. It was a tiny family ceremony, which included Joe and me and Steve's kids, Jennifer, Brady, and Daniel. The three of us were to move into Steve's house, and since I liked Steve's kids and house and in-ground pool, that was fine with me. Joe and I would leave for our annual Dad and Joyce summer, which is what we'd been doing since they'd come back from Europe, and we'd return before school to Blended Family #2, with our stuff already moved into the new house.

After a summer spent with Dad, Joyce (a.k.a. Mom), Brett, who was now a toddler, and our new baby half-brother Bryan, we returned to Florida to what turned out to be a tense, awkward living arrangement. The stepsiblings were pissed that they had to help move our belongings in—Steve was King Handyman, and rarely hired anyone to do anything. But Daniel graciously gave up his room to me and moved into the formal living room with Joe. The star-crossed parents were so smitten with each other while they dated that I don't think they realized how hard it was going to be to merge five kids in one house.

Stepdad #2 turned out to be the exact opposite of Don—a hyper-involved, type-A control freak—and that didn't gel with my freewheeling high-school-girl-about-town lifestyle. Steve, who resembles a cross between Burt Reynolds and Saddam Hussein, viewed five kids as indentured servants who were at his beck and call for anything from mulching to mowing. And if we didn't toe the line, there was hell to pay.

If we really pissed him off, we'd all have to line up, military style, and he'd shout humiliating, tedious questions at us like, "How old are you? And what do you pay for in this house? Who pays all the bills in this house? Who puts food on the table?"

After one particular degrading hour had ended, and he'd marched out of the room, I looked over at my three stepsiblings and observed, "Your father's an asshole." They all looked back at me and nodded. Brady shrugged, "I know."

I spent the rest of my high school career being frequently grounded, because my married mother and her husband had a lot more time and inclination to interfere with my drunken social life. I was outraged, because I thought it was incredibly unfair that my mom suddenly changed all the rules just because it suited her lifestyle. I felt oppressed by this man who had obviously missed all his classes in how to be a good stepparent, and I was angry with Mom for not shielding us from him.

I wasn't the only one who didn't dig the new living arrangements: Daniel moved in with his mom, Steve's first wife, who lived nearby. Brady eventually followed him. Joe moved in with our dad, who was now stationed in New Jersey, to finish out his school year, but he returned the following fall. Jennifer graduated from high school and left for college, and I followed suit a year later. I couldn't wait to get out.

Meanwhile, Dad and Joyce had increased their brood to three: they'd had a daughter named Kristin when I was fifteen. My dad, who loves orderliness, despite not being very orderly himself, was once cleaning up the toys that were strewn all over the living room, mumbling something about never even wanting children to begin with. I found this extremely funny at the time; he's now reached retirement age, and two of his five kids are still in high school.

Dad often seems just beyond reach, and it feels as though he's preoccupied with something else when we talk on the phone. In my dad's house, the squeaky wheel gets the oil, and Brett, Bryan, and Kristin's constant demands for attention gradually pushed Joe and me into the background. Our lives and interests seem to play second fiddle to those of the triumvirate, as I jokingly like to refer to them, since they rule the roost. And our half-siblings don't seem to be all that interested in really getting to know Joe or me.

Dad's first marriage is a skeleton in their Cleaver family closet. After nearly twenty-five years, Joyce still seems to struggle with the fact that Dad was married to someone else before he was married to her. And now what has evolved is that my brother and I have no defined identity within his second family. We aren't peers to our half-siblings, nor are we authority figures. We are electrons, forever destined to orbit their family nucleus.

SAM FLEW TO NEW YORK ON A FIANCÉ'S VISA that I'd secured for him. The visa granted us ninety days to decide whether we wanted to get married. If we decided against it, Sam would have no choice but to leave the United States, and since neither of us had enough money to travel back and forth, it would realistically be the end of our relationship.

He moved into my studio apartment near Gramercy Park, which I shared with my patient, understanding gay roommate Rob. Our living situation resembled a bad sitcom. My relationship with Sam quickly turned manic-depressive, due to the stress of the situation. We hated each other one day and slept together the next, and Rob spent lots of time in a local diner, reading and drinking coffee, in order to escape our squabbling. Each day the looming green-card wedding deadline crept nearer.

My mom knew what was going on between Sam and me, but she stayed calm and objective. She later told me she had been extremely worried and stressed out, but she figured hysterics or objections wouldn't help the situation. I kept my father in the dark, as he wasn't crazy about Sam to begin with. Dad has always been big on superficial first impressions—it must be his military background—and my cigarette-smoking, longhaired, holey-jeaned boyfriend didn't exactly have the Wally Cleaver charm.

Once, in my early twenties, I announced to my dad as we were driving that I didn't ever want a big wedding. He exclaimed, "Of course you do. Every girl wants a white wedding." I felt he was attempting to cram me into a conservative, stereotypical mold that he and my mother had themselves never fit into, and his comment made me all the more determined to thumb my nose at convention.

We got married at City Hall in Manhattan, on December 28—the ninetieth day of Sam's visa. I was happy with the prospect of a quiet, tiny wedding, as I'd never fancied the prospect of spending an entire year matching napkin colors to bridesmaids' dresses and working out conflict-free seating plans for my extended family. It always seemed like a waste of time and money.

The morning of the ceremony, I sat in our studio, feeling scared and slightly sick, while Sam was down on Fourteenth Street at a cheap jewelry shop, picking up our wedding bands, which were being sized. Mine was a $15 sterling-silver band that had "Made in Mexico" engraved on the inside. Sam's ring, also sterling silver, eventually turned his finger slightly green. I wore a cream-colored velvet A-line dress that I'd bought with my employee discount from Banana Republic, where I moonlighted for extra spending money. My mom paid for it.

We took the subway downtown to City Hall, where four of our friends met us—none of our family members were present, as we hadn't given them enough notice to be there. After the ceremony, I was swept by a massive sense of relief, a feeling that I'd just done the right thing, even though we still hadn't defined the nature of our relationship.

The wedding party crammed into a Mazda, and we headed for a bar in Chelsea for champagne and hors d'oeuvres. We had a great time, and we were relaxed—no constant scrutiny, no elaborate ritual. Sam and I stayed at the Gramercy Park Hotel on our wedding night, three blocks from our apartment, and Rob, grateful that we weren't in the studio with him, sent over a bottle of champagne.

A week after we got married, we were lying in bed, and Sam told me he was in love with me. I replied, "Well, that's a good thing, because I'm in love with you, too."

He and I tried to avoid the trappings of a traditional marriage, but ironically we took the form of a nuclear family anyway—and to our surprise, we're happy. While we work really hard to maintain a stable marriage, we've satisfied our need for a nontraditional life by moving; we've lived in eight apartments in three different countries in seven years.

And after five years together, Sam and I decided that we were ready to have a child, which we both viewed as the ultimate commitment to each other. Georgina was born in September 2000, and she was named after Sam's brother and my grandfather. Divorce will never be an option for me, and I cringe when I think about the havoc it would wreak on our now one-year-old daughter's life.

I don't know whether we loved each other all along and just never admitted it or whether we just made the decision to love each other, the way that some partners in arranged marriages might. But despite the ever-present atmosphere of divorce I grew up in, I do believe that love can endure if you give it room to evolve. I learned this from my father's parents—my true relationship role models—who continued to love each other, through wars and illnesses and affairs and children and travels, for nearly sixty years.

We have recently moved back to England, to a small historic market town in East Anglia, near Sam's parents, who have been married for over thirty years. As much as I love and admire them, I have no plans to call them Mom and Dad, as there have been too many people that I have felt pressure to address that way.

We are attempting to put down roots. I suspect it will be difficult and strange to stay in one place, as I have never been shown how. But I suppose that familiarity with impermanence has made the inevitable changes that life brings a bit less daunting. I want to give my daughter the stability and predictability that I never had, in a slow-paced setting rich in tradition and culture. I have chosen to alter the course that my parents set, look to my grandparents, and leave behind my revolving-door childhood in the pursuit of an antique solid oak door of adulthood.

THE MISSING

Ava Chin

MY FATHER LEFT US WHEN MY MOTHER was pregnant with me, and for many years I searched for clues of him. These were the only tangible objects he left behind: a faded black-and-white photograph of him circa 1969, smiling widely, seated in a rocking chair at my grandparents' house—an image later burned by my mother with a kitchen match when he refused to pay child support; a stuffed koala bear, presented to my mother in the early days of their courtship, with black plastic paws and a silver chain around its neck, which I slept with and drooled on as a child until the fake fur matted into hard lumps under my mouth; the sexy, diamond-cut engagement ring I had never before seen on my mother's slim finger, shined the day she sold it for less than its true value in order to pay the rent; a simple gold cross presented to me by my father's mother when I was an infant, devoid of decoration, hung on a tiny gold chain, and stored away in a plain white box. Though I have had it for many years, I have still never worn it.

I TRIED MANY TIMES TO VISUALIZE what my father looked like, but there was no tangible image to grab hold of, besides the burned photograph, which didn't exist anymore except in my memory. All that remained were leftover feelings of hatred, anger, and betrayal from my mother's family; a cold silence whenever his name was mentioned; a few disapproving looks; and the perceptible feeling that some secretly felt sorry for me despite my good grades, creativity, and thin-girl prettiness. It was a wound I carried with me through my teenage years, and into my twenties, dating boys who couldn't stop my pain and who eventually left defeated by my past. It was the wound that made me a writer, according to one professor in college, and I wielded it like a trophy that doubled as a weapon whenever anyone got too close.

Like many abandoned children, I created an elaborate fantasy about how I might one day meet my father, which changed and shifted through the years like my own developing body. In the earliest version, from a childhood informed by too much film and television, he would be laid prostrate on his deathbed and call for me, much like Pharaoh did for Moses in *The Ten Commandments*. He'd repeat my name insistently until his final breath.

In another version, I'd arrive unannounced to a family function at one of those Hong Kong–style banquet halls in Chinatown; I would be well dressed and half a foot taller than I actually grew to be. I'd dramatically throw aside the veil that covered my face, and surprise everyone by revealing myself as his daughter. No one would be able to dispute it, one look at me would be confirmation enough (I was reminded constantly by my mother's family that I looked "exactly like him").

In yet another version—imagined in my early post-collegiate days when I volunteered as a labor organizer in Chinatown—I would be abducted by gang members controlled by my father's well-connected family and we'd meet face-to-face, father and daughter. He'd be shocked, angry at his thugs, and embarrassed before setting me free. We'd cry, embrace, and catch up on lost years. (This I call the "Mob Princess" version.)

Though the details varied from year to year, from version to version, the central story line was always the same: repentant and ashamed, he would beg forgiveness and recognize me as the long-lost valued daughter he'd so actively overlooked. But the real events as they played out that led to my finding him were actually quieter, humbler, and more dramatic than I could ever have anticipated.

THE DETAILS BEHIND MY PARENTS' MEETING are infamous in our family history. The setting was New York's Chinatown in the late 1960s. My father, the first son in an important Chinese-American family, was the number-two lawyer in the community. He had political aspirations and, at the time when he met my mother, was seeking to run for the state assembly as a Democrat. He was separated from his first wife, a biracial beauty from Beijing, and had two daughters from this marriage. My mother, who was vivacious and also very beautiful, had just been crowned Miss Chinatown. She had a master's degree and was an elementary school teacher. Their sudden relationship was passionate and disastrous, like most relationships between politicians and beauty queens. He was older—thirty-six to her twenty-three—and closer to my grandparents' age than to hers. My mother was enthralled with him, indeed the legends of my father's charm are undeniable, even by those most disapproving of his actions. He owned a popular after-hours club on Bleecker Street in the West Village that some still remember to this day, and if you ask him about it, he can rattle off stories about Jimi Hendrix and Janis Joplin who used to frequent the bar as their post-gig hangout. Though my mother doesn't like to talk about their relationship, according to my grandmother, he did the proverbial sweeping her off her feet, and they were soon engaged to be married.

The rest of the story is rather blurry, but this is what I have gathered, and given what I now know about relations between men and women, seems to make the most sense. While engaged, they became pregnant with me. My mother, who wanted a child, was overjoyed. My father, who already had children, was not. According to my grandmother, he pressured her to get an abortion. This being 1969, and abortion illegal, she refused. Sometime after realizing that he couldn't change her mind, he shut off as men sometimes do—seemingly without feeling or outward signs of remorse. He said he no longer loved her. I believe that he fell in love with another woman. Falling in love with other women while he was already involved in a committed relationship would be a running motif in my father's life, but my mother wasn't yet privy to that information.

Pregnant and ashamed, my mother ran away from her family, and for several days her two older brothers searched for her, through Flushing, Kew Gardens, and Jamaica, Queens. My grandmother, who herself came from an influential Chinese banking family, and was born in this country and raised with money and the church in her bones, demanded a meeting with my father. He agreed to meet her with his lawyer. There must have been several hours of negotiating, which I can only imagine: my father, lean, in his ubiquitous suit, arguing that the disgrace would taint his career, his lawyer listening, giving occasional legal advice; my small grandmother, usually so accommodating, resolute and firm as she defended not only her daughter, but her family's reputation as well. She would later profess to a hatred of all lawyers that I had assumed was omnipresent, but that I now realize must have been the result of this meeting.

Finally, they came to an agreement: there would be a brief marriage, followed by a quick divorce. According to my grandmother, my father dramatically swore he would never lay eyes on the child as long as he lived. In that respect, unlike the broken engagement and the promise of love everlasting he promised to my mother and the two other wives after her, he was almost true to his word. Aside from the time in which my mother visited him with me, an infant in her arms, the next time I was to meet him would be when I was twenty-seven years old.

MY MOTHER HAD A DIFFICULT TIME RAISING ME, and not just because she was a single mother. Being a beautiful woman was an asset most of the time but could occasionally be a liability. She had been crowned Miss Chinatown and Miss Queen of Spring by the time she was twenty-two, and was used to drawing great attention long before she met my father. In that way that all beautiful people have, she grew accustomed to the world prostrating itself at her feet. She was smart and good-looking, and she had high expectations of what life had in store for her. So when my father so purposefully pulled the rug from under her, she was shocked and angry.

To support us, she taught in Bushwick, Brooklyn, for fifteen years, where she gradually grew strict and tough. Her vivacious openness transformed into a booming voice and a no-nonsense attitude. She raised me alone on her teacher's salary, and when my father refused to pay child support, she took him to court time and time again. These periods were characterized by taking days off from work and a bitterness I felt was inadvertently directed toward me. Every year it was the same: I would come home to find her laid out in bed with a migraine, begging me to be quiet and to leave her alone.

Her anger and disappointment toward my father was assuaged by material consumption. She obsessively window-shopped at fancy Manhattan stores, vowing that she would one day own what she could not afford then. She liked to collect objects en masse. First, it was Indian turquoise jewelry—necklaces and bracelets, which she wore every day in clunky layers; then Chinese cloisonné vases and matchboxes began to clutter her shelves, followed by redheaded Hummel statuettes with porcelain dogs pulling down their pants; silver mesh handbags adorned doorknobs and mirrors, and American matchboxes with imprints of angels gathered dust. My mother's apartment was a collection of rare items, ranging from schlocky to chic, that only she and I knew about. No one was ever invited to our apartment, and being fearful of her mood swings, I was reluctant to bring friends over.

We grew up more like two sisters sharing a two-bedroom apartment rather than mother and daughter. At night, she sometimes went out drinking and dancing with her friends or spent endless hours on the phone. Sometimes I threw a fit just so she'd pay attention to me. I knew all of her boyfriends from the time I was a toddler, and she had to admit that I could easily discern the jerks from the nice ones. She could be a vicious fighter, prone to yelling and shoving, whereas I developed a passive-aggressive style, often shutting off and suppressing my anger. We remained that way for many years, her angry and vocal, me silent and seething. It was harder for me to see the role I played in it then.

Sometimes it was fun having a young mother. She had a loud, infectious laugh, and often took me to R-rated movies. When I was a teenager, my friends were impressed that she loved R&B music, and knew the latest hairstyles and clothing trends. She allowed me to stay out late, and never raised a fuss about my dating because, after all, she was dating too.

Though I toyed with the fantasy of meeting my father, I never told her about it. That she could possibly understand was unrealistic, and I felt, too much to ask for. So I kept silent about it and prayed she wouldn't be too upset when I finally did find the courage to meet him.

My grandmother was the only one who talked to me about my father:

He was a charmer, that one, a real louse. He came from a big family, a huge family, you should see how many cousins he has. You have two sisters, one adopted. It's a shame they never bothered to look you up.

It was a terrible burden on your mother, you know. She was never the same after what he did to her.

He could have helped out. He had the money. I'm quite sure he supported his other daughters.

But he was only looking for a good time. He used your mother, then threw her away.

What can you do? Things worked out the way they did.

In the summer of 1997, I met my sisters for the first time. They were the daughters from my father's first marriage. Meeting them was the realization of a long-held fantasy—growing up an only child, I had always wanted sisters. The one closest in age to me, Kristine, was small, lively, and personable. She worked in magazine publishing like I did (she was a photo editor at *Condé Nast Traveler*), and I felt an instant kinship with her. Then there was Nadine, who was pleasant but distant; she'd known all of the stepmothers (three) and numerous girlfriends, and already had another half-sister and a host of ex-stepsisters. She had the wary air of the disinterested that either meant she was very interested or else really couldn't care less. When you've been exposed to a parent's numerous failed relationships ever since you were ten, I suppose you learn not to get too close.

At our first meeting together we had dinner at a French bistro on Twenty-Third Street. I felt light-headed, almost giddy. Being with my two older sisters gave a sense of sibling connectedness that I had never felt before; it meant more to me than I think they realized. I liked the familiarity they had with each other, the friendly banter, the mutual support. They said that they had told "Dad" about me and that he was very excited to meet. They wanted to know when I was going to call him. I was polite, but gently pushed the questions aside. Thankfully, they let me change the subject.

I was surprisingly resistant to the idea of meeting him. Now that I was so close, something very stubborn within me was refusing to do it, and I wasn't exactly sure why. Before, I had always had the fear that he'd reject me. (The idea of this type of double rejection is something that even now makes me shudder to think about.) But the fact that he had expressed a desire to meet took that fear away, and instead, I was left with anger. Where had he been all that time, and why hadn't *he* come to meet *me*? Why did I have to be the one who took the risk and approach him? Wasn't he the adult? Shouldn't he be the one to get in touch? I debated back and forth like this for several months.

I felt, in a way, that my very identity was being threatened. I was, after all, the girl who had never met her father. I was someone everyone felt sorry for, but admired for being strong. It allowed me to feel righteous about the harshness of the world, to feel that I was somehow better for dealing so well with the burden. I had grown very used to this chip I'd had on my shoulder for so long. I wasn't quite ready to give it up.

WHEN I WAS A CHILD, MY CLOSE FRIENDS would ask if I hated my father.

I used to think it was an odd question. *Hate* was too strong an emotion for a man I had never met. Whenever I thought of him, I drew a complete blank. Like a big white space in the middle of a sentence signifying a missing word—a word like "love" or "life" or "anger" or "pain." "Father" was synonymous with "missing" or "hole." "Father" to me meant "absence of father."

"I don't hate him," I said many times throughout my childhood, my adolescence, and even well into my twenties. I wasn't sure who my father was—the burned photograph, the koala bear, the engagement ring, the tiny cross. "How can you hate someone you don't even know?"

I felt nothing toward him but a cold, almost Zen-like distance. It was rather like facing the impenetrability of a blank sheet of paper right before you started a new story and found the words to mark up the page.

THE PERSON WHO CAME CLOSEST to filling the role of surrogate dad was my grandfather—a big, boisterous man with a voice so deep and resonant it could make the hairs on the back of your neck stand on end. He was tall and very handsome in a film-starrish way, and I used to watch, fascinated, as women flirted with him. He was a bartender and manager of a restaurant, and when I was in kindergarten, I would sit and watch the locals drink scotch and bourbon and listen to my grandfather's easy banter. He had a sense of humor that could make even unfunny jokes amusing. He was a very good bartender and a very good grandfather, and the two are not usually inclusive. By the time I met him, he was in his fifties and had apparently settled down a great deal.

Being the last person to emigrate from China in 1938, my grandfather was the only one in the family who spoke with a Chinese accent. He had village tendencies like trapping pigeons under milk crates or catching insects between his fingers. He spoke with a country dialect my grandmother didn't want me to learn, so we got along through half-gestures and phrases that only we understood. Although he had other granddaughters with his last name—whereas mine by Chinese custom indicated that I belonged to some *other* family—the only photograph he kept on his dresser was of me, aged four, in a pink dress with a beribboned front, smiling widely, my front teeth barely grown in.

In the months between meeting my sisters and debating over whether or not to call my father, my grandfather was diagnosed with cancer. It was the first time I had to deal with the impending death of a loved one and it literally changed everything. I started to seriously contemplate the idea of having children. For most of my twenties, I concentrated on my work and career, going through boyfriends after a few years or even a few months. In New York this was considered normal. We were too busy and too broke to be thinking of marriage or children. And it was hard enough finding someone who wanted to be monogamous, much less someone who was willing to get serious and settle down. I still remember getting the key to my then-boyfriend's front door after a solid year of dating, and considering it a huge accomplishment at the time.

My grandfather's diagnosis was a revelation. I was twenty-seven and I wanted to have a family one day. Though I had always assumed that I would be a single mother like my mom, I realized that it was possible to find someone who wanted the same things. Thinking about the future generation made it simple. If I was going to be a good parent, then I needed to find out what happened between my own parents. I needed to answer the biggest question that had eluded me for so many years, and for that, I needed to know who my father was.

MAKING THAT PHONE CALL was the hardest thing I had ever done. I was shaking when I dialed the office number that my sister had given me. It rang a few times before someone picked up. The voice on the other end was shaky and hollow, like wind rattling through an old house. My father was ten years younger than my grandfather, but I was surprised that he sounded much older. After I introduced myself, there was an awkward pause. (As it turned out, his third wife has the same name, and he was struggling to figure out who I was.)

Then I heard the recognition in his voice, followed by the expression of slight irritation over why it had taken me so long to call, which I found annoying (after all, I had been waiting for him my entire life). I wanted to meet soon, while I still had the courage, and was relieved when he agreed to meet a few days later for dinner in Chinatown. He asked if my sisters could join us. I had the sense he wanted to hide behind them if things got too harried with me, so I suggested they meet us later. "I'd like to meet with you alone first."

He agreed smoothly enough, and we confirmed we would meet at his office on Pell Street. For the first time, it would be just the two of us. One on one.

I DREAMED TWO NIGHTS LATER that my father was trying to kill me.

In the dream, I was in a strange, unfamiliar apartment. I couldn't see him, but he was hiding in the shadows with a knife. I woke up terrified and alone, in the middle of the night in my own Brooklyn bedroom. I tried to calm down and listen for any strange noises, but all I could hear was the rush of traffic over the sound of my own breathing.

HE WAS DARK-HAIRED AND DISTINGUISHED. He wore a tailored suit and was handsome in that way much older men can be. We met at his office on 3 Pell Street, which I'd passed numerous times before but had never noticed, despite his name on the plaque emblazoned on the wall. His handshake was strong for his lean build, and he seemed tall, though I realized he was, in fact, not much taller than I was as we walked up the stairs to the second floor office.

His office was tiny and spare. There was a front vestibule, where the secretary had once sat, but which now, in my father's semi-retirement, was empty. Covering the walls were black-and-white photographs of him shaking hands with Bobby Kennedy and Donald Manus, the Queens borough president with whom he had shared an office in Jamaica, and who later committed suicide in the 1980s. By his desk were the campaign shots of my father, in his late thirties, taken around the time I was born. His hair was rakishly wavy, and he looked serene and confident in his picture above a row of stars. Along the bookshelves and on his desk, were framed photos of my sisters when they were children—sitting on boats, or at the beach house on the New Jersey shore. There were snapshots of former wives and his stepdaughter. I felt some envy, for this life I never had, but these feelings didn't really come out until later, after I had processed all the new information. I was still struggling with my father as a tangible reality.

We sat and talked for a few minutes, and I searched his face for traces of myself. I had always been told I looked like him, and my sister had said we had the same high forehead. There were similarities, the same red-brown eyes with the propensity for dark circles; the same shaped nose, face, and indeed, the same forehead. But, while I was prepared to see physical similarities, I was not expecting to recognize similarities in outward temperament. As he guardedly told me about his life, his run in politics, his wives after my mother, I noticed it. A certain carefulness of speech. A purposefully calm exterior. He had the same way of talking that I did when I was on the extreme defensive. Later, I would see that we even had the same way of walking.

Instead of making me happy, however, these realizations just made me angry. I did not want to admit I had inherited more than just similar looks from this man who had abandoned my mother. Did that mean that I had inherited other tendencies from him too? My mother always said that we sounded alike, especially when I was being "obnoxious," but I always dismissed these claims as being based solely on bitterness. Could my manner and personal demeanor, which I considered entirely my own, be from him? And if so, what other traits had I inherited? A charming but flawed personality? A cavalier attitude and a roving eye? An unwillingness to settle down and take responsibility for my actions?

We left his office a few minutes later to go to dinner. Walking through the crowded narrow streets of old Chinatown, he was very much on the defensive, even as he leaned forward a little, casually pointing out buildings associated with the family. The red brick apartment building where

he grew up, on the curved foot of Mott Street. The Chin family Associ-
ation a few blocks away where my cousin still lived, with its red lettered
sign in large Chinese characters over the door. He was making small
pleasantries, but didn't ask about me or why I had wanted to meet, fearing an attack. So I purposely asked him questions about his life, centered
around the time that I was born, to put him at ease. He rambled on as
we crossed Canal Street, speaking more enthusiastically than he perhaps
was feeling.

We entered a tiny restaurant, where he knew the owner, and were
seated near the front. It was the first time I had heard his side of the story,
and as you would expect from Chinatown's number-two lawyer, he
spoke very eloquently about his life. Around the time I was born, he was
in his late thirties, and his career was in full bloom. There was his thriv-
ing practice, which benefited from his being one of the few Chinese-
American lawyers in the city. He represented our family's *tong*—which
was one of the first family associations in the country and directly
involved in New York's bloody *tong* wars of the 1910s and 1920s. There
was his club, Nobody's, and the celebrity rock stars who'd hung out
there. His political career was promising—the family had clout, and he
was popular in the Lower East Side. But when a group of radical leftists
split the democratic vote, he lost the election to the incumbent; he was
certain he would have won, if not for their interference. (When I asked
what platform he had run on, he said without the slightest trace of guilt
and in spite of the fact I was sitting right before him, that he "firmly
believed in abortion and a woman's right to choose.") He told me about
his third wife, Lisa, a sexy stewardess he'd married and divorced twice.
They used to compete in international hustle competitions in Hong Kong
and China. There was his stepdaughter, Sheila, who grew up with my
sisters, spending her summers out on the Jersey shore.

He talked at great length throughout dinner. He was quite pleased
with the colorfulness of his life, and was reminiscing fondly, when about
three-quarters of the way through our meal, I decided to tell him how I

felt. I wasn't sure if he could handle it, but I took a deep breath and tried to talk as deliberately and truthfully as possible.

I told him that all he accomplished around 1969 and 1970 was fascinating—the campaign, the club, the different women. My being born at that time, I understood, may have been just one more facet of a period for him that he'd forgotten or quite simply overlooked. I paused for a moment. He was looking at me earnestly from across the table, his hands lowered, the tip of his chopsticks touching his plate. I had what I wanted—his full, undivided attention.

"But for me, that time you weren't there meant everything."

WE HAD A SHORT BUT GLORIOUS getting-to-know-you period.

For my twenty-eighth birthday that year, he joined me and about a dozen of my friends, including my best friend Leslie, at a dinner party. The present he gave me was a heavy teakwood sculpture, made by his father, and wrapped in long white paper. It was an elongated carving of a grandfather with a heavy beard, carrying a long staff in one hand, and shielding a grandchild with the other. It was heavy in my hands and I had barely said thank you before the blur of my own tears clouded my vision.

I was holding something the grandfather I had never known had made, and I couldn't stop crying. The mixed emotions were sharp and intense: sheer happiness and pain, joy and anger, and most of all an overriding feeling of relief. Psychologists call this phenomenon "shrinking," and it occurs when athletes who have been training for years finish a big performance and suddenly burst into tears—you see this sometimes during the Olympics. My friends watched—some understanding, others embarrassed—and, according to Leslie, my father, who was sitting next to me, looked like he too was about to break down.

The irony was not lost on me that I was presented with a gift made by this grandfather I'd been estranged from, by the very person who had caused the estrangement in the first place. I was overjoyed but angry. No one could return that lost history, not even the very person who had taken it away from me. Beyond the sound of my own crying, I could hear the buzz of the restaurant, crowded on a Saturday evening. Everyone around me thought I was sad and upset, especially my father who was looking concerned and hesitantly patting my hand.

Really, I was the happiest I'd been in a long time.

I WISH I COULD SAY THAT WE CONTINUED to have a wonderful relationship, that we shared many rich father–daughter experiences together. Throughout the spring and summer of 1998 we were in touch—he bought me a share in my sister's summer house on Fire Island, and I spent some time with him and my sisters. I put the wooden grandfather carving on a special place on my bookshelf and dusted it often. But the next year, his girlfriend from Los Angeles, who was having drug problems, wanted to come to New York so they could be together, and he set her up in a rehab clinic in Manhattan.

My father, I was soon to learn, was like a child who could only focus on what was right in front of him at the moment: a truck, a stuffed animal, a daughter, it didn't matter. Like yesterday's toys we were interchangeable. He could only concentrate on one woman at a time, and when his girlfriend came to town, it meant that he wouldn't return my phone calls or my letters. For my sisters, who went through all of his many marriages and divorces, this was familiar terrain. Kristine, especially, verbally walked me through it.

In the end, my father engaged in a new set of dramas that upset his life *and* theirs: moving in with his girlfriend, catching pneumonia, moving back out when his girlfriend got violent (on withdrawal from crack and cocaine), moving back in when she became clean again. I wish that I could say that he was just having a midlife crisis, that it was a phase he would get over. But my father, who has married and divorced five times during the course of his life, is now seventy years old, and unlikely to change.

THE MOST REMARKABLE, UNEXPECTED OUTCOME of meeting my father was how it affected my relationship with my mother.

We were in the car when I told her about meeting him, on our way to visiting my grandfather. "Do you like him?" she asked, clutching the wheel as we sped through the old neighborhood in Kew Garden Hills, down 150th Street, past all the new construction. When I hesitated, she said, "It's okay, you can say that you do."

She was open to listening to how I felt about him, and his scattered presence in my life. Instead of being angry as I'd feared all those years, she actually seemed relieved. Her hands visibly relaxed on the wheel. Later, she promised to kill him if he hurt me.

As time went by, I noticed the unmistakable change in her. It was as if the air had been let out of a pressurized tank. She was calmer, happier, and somehow more liberated. She seemed more beautiful to me now than I had ever seen her before, even in her twenties and thirties. I realized that her anger had somehow connected her to him, and for all these years it had also held her back. It was only after I had met him that she could finally let go.

We have talked about her resentment over raising me alone, and how her anger toward him sometimes trickled down to me. It was wrong, she finally admitted, to burn his photograph in front of me when I was so young. She was sorry that she had done it. But she was never ashamed of me, as I'd feared for so many years. The shame and bitterness she felt was over being a single mother, not of being *my* mother.

As the years progressed, I kept her informed about my father. His errant ways, and our unsteady relationship. His Houdini "now you see me, now you don't" behavior. How I was slowly coming to accept it all.

It was the same old thing, I told her over the phone a little while ago. We were really better off without him.

SOMETIMES, I WONDER HOW IT WILL BE FOR ME. If having two parents who were more in love with being in love has indeterminately affected my own chances of weathering marriage. Am I doomed to repeat the patterns of the past? Take away the nurture component of the old "nature vs. nurture" paradigm and consider for a moment the possibilities of genetic determination: Do two fools for love, blindly fumbling around in the dark, beget another fool—as two blond parents are prone to having a blond child? Do two intellectuals bring forth a spate of ivy-leaguers? Do two racists naturally beget a racist, or is it possible for them to produce an ardent liberal? Can two musical illiterates bless the world with a musical genius?

Now in the third year of knowing each other, I still have very mixed feelings about my father. For my mother and her family it is easier: to her, he is the charming and dynamic man who left and broke her heart; for my grandmother, he is the man who ruined her daughter. For me, it is much more complex. I have to contend with the reality that the man who left my mother pregnant to jet-set across the continents with another woman, is in fact, my own father. And that's something I will always have to negotiate, even as I try to deal with the past and toy with the idea of having a family of my own one day.

Part of becoming an adult, I am learning, is shouldering the responsibilities of being a daughter or a son. I keep thinking that I want to honor and respect this, despite the disappointment I feel about my father. I see him now only on rare occasions like Chinese New Year or Father's Day. And even when he forgets simple things, like my birthday or to call to see how I'm doing, I make an effort and phone him when too many months have gone by. Maybe a component of maturing is swallowing the kind of bitterness old Chinese ladies are always talking about. Maybe it means still being a good daughter, even when a parent isn't being a good parent.

I am happy that I met him. The tangible is always preferable to a myth, no matter how dramatic or grandiose. As novelist Mona Simpson wrote in *The Lost Father*, all anyone needs to do to reach god-like status is to walk out. Somewhere along the line, I became tired of mythologizing spare parts, looking for clues in misplaced objects and old photographs. And for the first time, I feel a range of conflicting emotions toward him that alternate between anger, pain, sorrow, and even a hint of tenderness.

Early on when I met my father, I asked him why he had married so many times. His answer was immediate, almost childlike in its logic. "You fall in love. You decide to marry. If it doesn't work out, you get a divorce." He made it sound so simple, like an if-then statement in basic mathematics. But I suspect not even he truly believes this, that you can walk away so unaffected, debt-free.

ABOUT THE CONTRIBUTORS

MATT BRIGGS is the author of *The Remains of River Names* (Black Heron Press) and a collection of short stories, *Misplaced Alice* (String-Town). His fiction has appeared in *The Mississippi Review*, *Northwest Review*, *ZYZZYVA*, and elsewhere. He lives in Seattle with his wife and daughter and is writing a novel.

JAMES BROWNING lives in Annapolis and is the executive director of the Maryland chapter of Common Cause, a nonprofit organization. He is currently working on a novel.

AYANA BYRD, twenty-eight, is a Brooklyn-based journalist whose work has appeared in *Vibe*, *Rolling Stone*, *Essence*, *Honey*, and *Paper* magazines. She has recently completed a chapter on black female subjectivity in rap music for the feminist anthology *Future Perfect*, and is a contributor to an upcoming book by *Vibe* magazine on women and hip hop. Byrd has appeared on C-Span and National Public Radio, and on numerous panels, including Harvard University's Black Arts Festival and Barnard College's Scholar and the Feminist. She is the coauthor of *Hair Story: Untangling the Roots of Black Hair in America* (St. Martin's Press).

Seattle-based writer and editor NOVELLA MERCEDES CARPENTER, twenty-eight, writes for *The Stranger*, and has contributed essays to *The Unsavvy Traveler* (Seal) and *The Stranger's Guide to Seattle* (Sasquatch). She coauthored *Don't Jump, the Northwest Winter Blues Survival Guide* (Sasquatch), and is currently gathering essays for an anthology about the back-to-the-land movement.

It was her mother's gift of a journal that sparked Montana-born writer PEPPUR CHAMBERS's writing career at age ten. She is currently developing a book of short stories, titled *Midwestern Girl*, based on her first year living in New York City. Her published essay "Texas" first appeared in *TellSpin* magazine and has been excerpted here in "Three-Way."

AMY CONWAY is an editor and writer in New York City. She currently lives in Westchester with her husband and son.

PAULA GILOVICH, twenty-nine, is the author of *Plastiques: An Exhibit of Sex Toys During Wartime* and the cofounder of the publishing collective 10th Avenue East. She is a contributing writer for *The Stranger* and is the coeditor of *The Stranger's Guide to Seattle* (Sasquatch). She has contributed to *Allure Magazine* and the *New York Times*.

Poet DOUGLAS GOETSCH is the author of *Nobody's Hell* (Hanging Loose Press), *Wherever You Want* (Pavement Saw Press), and *What's Worse* (Aldrich Museum). His work has appeared in numerous journals including *The Iowa Review*, *Ploughshares*, *Poetry*, and *American Poetry: The Next Generation* (Carnegie Mellon Press). Goetsch's honors include the Paumanok Award, a Prairie Schooner Reader's Choice Award, and two recent Pushcart Prize nominations. A New York City high school teacher for many years, he currently teaches creative writing to incarcerated teens in the South Bronx.

SERENA KIM, twenty-eight, lives in Brooklyn with her boyfriend and is a senior editor at *Vibe* magazine. She moved from Los Angeles to New

York in 1995 to work in the music industry, and has written for *The Source*, *The Fader*, *XXL*, and other hip hop media outlets. She hopes to become a full-time creative writer.

AARON KUNIN, twenty-eight, lives in Baltimore, where he teaches film and curates the Mellon Poetry Seminar at Johns Hopkins. He's working on a Ph.D. in the English department at Duke University, where he specializes in the Renaissance. His poetry has appeared or is forthcoming in *Fence*, *The Germ*, and *Jubilat*. He also writes book reviews for *Rain Taxi*.

KELLY MURPHY MASON grew up in southern New England. She studied writing at Harvard College and the University of Michigan, where she won a Hopwood Award. Her work has appeared in *The Washington Post Book World*, *Slate*, *The Week*, and *Beliefnet*. She lives in a Brooklyn brownstone with a tomcat named Tucker.

MICHELLE PATIENT is a freelance writer and editor who has contributed to *Entertainment Weekly*, *Architecture*, and *Photo District News* magazines. A compulsive mover and avid traveler, she has previously lived her adult life in New York, London, and Barbados. She currently resides in Saffron Walden, England, with her husband Sam and their one-year-old daughter Georgina.

Writer JILL PRILUCK has contributed stories to the *New York Times*, *ARTnews*, *Salon*, *Vibe* magazine, and others.

Poet JEN ROBINSON is the author of *For Conifer Fanatics* (Soft Skull Press) and *Darwin In Argentina* (Mundungus) and coauthor of *Dictionary Of Useful Phrases* (The Gift). Her work has appeared in numerous journals and on the television series *Dawson's Creek*. She is the puzzle editor of *Lungfull!* magazine and has performed at venues such as the Nuyorican Poets Café, the St. Mark's Poetry Project, and Blue Books at New College in San Francisco. She received her bachelor's degree from Barnard College and an MFA from Brooklyn College. She lives in Queens.

JOHN STINSON's fiction has appeared in *Glimmer Train Stories*, *Chicago Review*, *Berkeley Fiction Review*, and the *Baltimore City Paper*. He is a graduate of Kenyon College and Johns Hopkins University.

ALEXANDRA WOLF, twenty-eight, was born and raised in Manhattan. She attended the University of Michigan, and she now lives in New York.